Lucas vs. The Green Machine

David Lucas

ALEXANDER Books

Founded 332 B.C.

a division of Creativity, Inc.

65 Macedonia Road
Alexander, NC 28701 USA
(704) 255-8719

Publisher: Ralph Roberts

Cover Design: **WorldComm**®

Executive Editor: Lorna Bolkey

Managing Editor: Carolyn Herrington

Editors: Lorna Bolkey, Josh Warren, Pat Hutchison Roberts

Interior Design and Electronic Page Assembly: WorldComm®

Printed in the United States of America

First Edition, Second Printing

10 9 8 7 6 5 4 3 2

Library of Congress Cataloging-in-Publication Data

Lucas, David, 1947-
      Lucas vs. the Green Machine / David Lucas.
             p. cm.
      Includes index.
      ISBN 1-57090-011-6
        1. Lucas, David, 1947-   --Trials, litigation, etc.   2. South Carolina Coastal Council--Trials, litigation, etc.   3. Eminent domain--South Carolina. Compensation (Law)--South Carolina.   5. Shore protection--Law and legislation--South Carolina. 6. Right of property--United States.   I. Title.
KF228.L83L83 1995
343.757'0252--dc20
[347.5703252]   95-12090
                                           CIP

Alexander Books—a division of Creativity, Inc.—is a full–service publisher located at 65 Macedonia Road, Alexander NC 28701. Phone (704) 252–9515 or (704) 255–8719 fax. For orders only: 1-800-472-0438. Visa and MasterCard accepted.

Contents

Preface

"Nor shall any person... be deprived of life, liberty, or property, without due process of law; nor shall private property be taken for public use, without just compensation."

—The Fifth Amendment of the *Constitution of the United States*

In 1989, when I filed the lawsuit that was to be known as *Lucas vs. South Carolina Coastal Council*, I had no idea the case would take on such national significance. Since winning in the U.S. Supreme Court in 1992, I have received hundreds, if not thousands, of letters and telephone calls from sympathetic Americans who have *their* own stories to share. A good number of these folks encouraged me to write this book. This, then, is the entire story told from my perspective in an attempt to end the disinformation campaign that opponents of property rights have been waging since the case was accepted by the U.S. Supreme Court.

My story is about an endangered species of American. An American from a hard working, rural background, who was able to live the American dream. Starting without privilege, money, or connections, this American son was able to succeed in the business world at a relatively early age and live a life far removed from the cotton fields and tobacco barns of his youth. That upbringing had prepared him for the challenges that he would face in a competitive world. He had great parents that were strict, but loving. He was all too familiar with the size 38 leather belt that his father used to punctuate his instructions from time to time. The hours spent on Sunday mornings in Saint Matthew Methodist Church certainly did add to the positive upbringing that he received. The neighbors and friends of his small community taught him many valuable lessons that he was able to use in his future life.

The first big challenge confronting me was how to pay for a college education. I was offered an athletic scholarship by the University of South Carolina to play football. Although at six feet six inches in height and only one hundred and eighty five pounds in weight, I was built more like a basketball player than a football player. I had no other way to pay for my education, so I thank-

fully accepted. I was so thin at the time, Lou Holtz
of Notre Dame fame, who was an assistant coach
at USC back then, nicknamed me "Twiggy." But
soon I gained some weight and some skill and was
even voted Honorable Mention All Atlantic Coast
Conference at defensive end. By playing against
major collegiate competition that usually out-
weighed me by up to one hundred pounds, I
learned that you can win against the odds and
the bigger players. Bigger is not always better. I
learned how to direct those bigger bodies away
from me to some harmless spot on the field. A
very important lesson that was to serve me well
and often in the future.

Times have changed. Individuals now find the
economic ladder has been jerked out of reach by
all levels of governments of this country, and the
American Dream is too often never realized. This
is the story of an American who was able to grasp
a rung on that ladder only to have his own government threaten his climb. If this were an isolated incident, this story would not have much
appeal. But, through unnecessary and oppressive
regulation, governments stifle and many times
destroy economic activity, wealth and individual
initiative.

If this trend continues and is not reversed, only
those with privilege, money, or connections will
be able to participate. This will surely result in

the ruination of our country and its liberties. The economic liberties and opportunities that have historically been open to all, regardless of one's circumstances, must not be diminished–just the opposite, they should be expanded.

This country is at a crossroads in its history. Do we continue on the present course that undermines individual liberty and initiative in quest of an elitist vision of a utopian society that has failed countless times in the past, or do we return to the path of individual freedom that our founding fathers blazed for us so long ago? The foundation of our freedom is the right to private property, and today, like so many of our other individual liberties, it is under attack from many different special interest groups and, yes, even our own governments. It is time for all who hold the constitution dear to rally to its defense. It would be wise for us to heed the words of Albert Einstein: *"The strength of the Constitution lies entirely in the determination of each citizen to defend it."* We must oppose those in government and private sector who would ignore the simple words of the Fifth Amendment every time it suits their narrow purpose. Each time an American's constitutional right to own and use his land is violated, it eventually affects every single man, woman and child in this country. We must unite in our efforts, and resist the onslaught of accumulated governmental powers. We must go to the ballot boxes, appeal to the courts, push legislation, and come to the support of our neighbors when they are set upon by misguided bureaucrats who attempt to confiscate their land. Look around carefully and you will find that it is probably occurring in your neighborhood to someone you know.

These fights are, often, time consuming, expensive, and tortuous. But in the end, they can be won. Our children deserve no less. The freedom that this country enjoys has been won and defended throughout our history by the blood, sweat and tears of Americans in wars and struggles at home and abroad. They have not sacrificed so dearly, for us to give up our birthright so easily. We must do our part to protect the Fifth Amendment, for it has allowed all other individual liberties to flourish. The recognition that private property sparks the flame of liberty is growing all over the world. We must ensure that the very nation that produced that flame continues to provide the intellectual fuel to keep it burning brightly.

We must return to a system of limited government. There are areas of our lives that should be off limits to *all* government intervention. This was the intention of the founders of our Republic. They understood that the more powerful a government becomes, the more liberty it will demand from its citizens. If left unchecked by its people, the government will not protect its citizens, but will oppress them. This unfortunate fact is as old as human civilization itself. Scheherezade in *The Arabian Nights*, written over one thousand years ago, makes this link between people and power: *"oppression hideth in every heart: power revealeth it and weakness concealeth it."* A government's power must never exceed the power of its people.

I have benefitted intellectually and spiritually since 1989 from the people that I have met because of this ordeal. Multitudes of Americans are fighting daily to insure that the Fifth Amendment to the Constitution remains vital and indispensable to our society. I now realize that my story is just another small chapter in the continuing struggle for life, liberty and the pursuit of happiness. This book is dedicated to my family for their unwavering support, and to the courageous men and women who have fought throughout America's history to protect and defend freedom for us all.

1
Bluegrass Not Green Grass

OR:

How I Got Myself Into This Mess

Columbia, South Carolina
Summer 1977

Willo was late. That made me nervous. I had never played a job like this before with a band, much less alone. This was not like our normal two man gig. Hell, anybody can have a few beers and then get up and pick and sing in front of your bar room buddies. They wouldn't know whether you were good or bad as long as you played loud. I had done plenty of that alright, but this kind of job was different. We were going to have to show some professionalism.

We had been asked to do some entertaining for the Governor of the great state of South Carolina. So, here we were in Columbia, at the Lace

House, an antebellum home that was right next door to the Governor's Mansion. The Lace House was used by the Governor for important state functions. It was beautiful and imposing, and tonight it would be crawling with the state's top political muckity-mucks.

Willo and I had actually rehearsed for this job. I had even gone to the trouble of learning some new chords on the guitar just for this gig. The hard part was trying to remember all of the words to all of the new songs that we had selected (notice that for this job we selected these songs, we didn't just pick'em). Of course, I didn't have a problem with remembering the words to the old standby stuff that everybody liked. Songs such as the Carter family's "Will the Circle Be Unbroken," or the Hank Williams' tune, "I Saw the Light," or even that old Roy Acuff favorite, "Wabash Cannonball," were easy for me to remember. I had heard my father and uncle play and sing them all the time as I was growing up back on the farm in Turkey Creek.

Those songs weren't the problem. It was those hard-core bluegrass tunes that caused my fingers to get lost in the middle of the song. Numbers like "Rocky Top" and "Fox on the Run" used minor chords—chords that, until we started trying to play those unfamiliar bluegrass tunes, I didn't even know existed. I sure was glad to see Mr. Willo

Collins stroll in with his big ol'wide grin and his black banjo case. Willo was a born ham and loved to perform anytime or any place for anybody willing to listen.

This was to be a real, for pay, formal job. Willo had performed professionally for many years, but I hadn't. They were going to actually pay us fifty bucks apiece. Now I know that wasn't much money. That was not the point. The point was that I was actually going to be paid for picking and singing for people that I didn't know. After tonight, I would be a paid entertainer. That was exciting to a lifelong Grand Old Oprey fan like me.

This was not going to be another small town talent contest in a little gym in front of the homefolks where first prize was ten silver dollars and an appearance on the local radio show on Saturday morning. Back in high school, I had done lots of those. Most of that audience would have already heard you sing in the school play or in your church choir on some special Sunday. That was hard enough to get used to, but this was in front of people who were mostly strangers, important political strangers at that.

I knew they would talk about you if you messed up. Once when I was a teenager, I sang a solo for my Saint Matthew Methodist church congregation. The hymn was "How Great Thou Art." When

LUCAS VS. THE GREEN MACHINE

I got to the first high note in the chorus, my voice broke. My Dad said it wouldn't have been so bad except for the terrible grimace I had made. I can still remember that grimace, it was a good one. Half the congregation took one look and ran for their lives.

After I got the cobwebs out of my voice and finally got the song going, I hit the rest of those high notes with ease, but I never forgot that embarrassing moment. Fortunately for me, the congregation had heard me do a much better job before, so they were kind. A few of the congregation that had fled for their lives even came back for the end of the song; but, I didn't know these people at the Governor's soiree and they didn't know me. If I made that awful screeching sound again with this crowd of politicos, I might get arrested.

Bad reviews could ruin one's whole week and a budding musical career. But we were prepared and I was confident that with Willo's great banjo and guitar playing, I could find the right tune and correct key at least part of the time. Besides, people in South Carolina generally liked traditional country songs with a little bluegrass thrown in.

Ken Allen had gotten me into this. My attorney and friend, Ken, was also a justice of the peace. My wife, Martha, and I had seen him often at Republican functions. He was very involved with the Republican party during this time and had been particularly active in the campaign to elect South Carolina's first Republican Governor since the days of reconstruction.

Ken's wife, Margo, had listened to us play at the beach many times before. Willo and I had been going down to Murrel's Inlet on weekends to do a little deep sea fishing. He was, in addition to being a great banjo player, an avid fisherman and hunter. People loved to hear him play, so he always carried his banjo with him. I think it was the same one that he had used to back up Pat Boone when Pat won the Ted Mack Amateur contest back in the fifties. At least that was his story and he's still sticking to it. Willo wears white buck shoes to this day in honor of that occasion.

Willo and I had been introduced by Johnny Ball, an old friend of mine and Willo's. Johnny and Willo had grown up together in Nashville, Tennessee. Johnny was from an old South Carolina family with roots going back to colonial days. Although Johnny and I weren't related, our families had crossed paths and interacted often during the past. We had a lot of cousins in common. After college, Johnny had moved back to South Carolina. Willo had recently gotten a divorce from his first wife back in Nashville, so he moved down to Columbia where his friend, Johnny, lived.

Johnny and I sold real estate together in Columbia and had gotten to know one another pretty well. Besides the family connections, we both shared a love for the great outdoors. This was the guy who had introduced me to deep sea fishing a few years before. Besides hunting and fishing, Johnny knew that I liked to play and sing country music. I could play the guitar and sing Hank Williams and Johnny Cash songs. I usually didn't get booed, and I felt that I could at least carry a tune. So Johnny had put Willo and me together to see if he could get some recognizable music from the match.

Willo began to teach me some bluegrass tunes. Soon we were spending a lot of time together picking and singing. Since Willo and I had music, hunting and fishing in common, we soon became good friends. Over the course of the next few years we began to pick and sing around Columbia and Murrell's Inlet for friends on a regular basis.

The deep sea fishing out of Murrel's Inlet was great. My college roommate, John D. Coleman, and I had bought a 27 foot Scotticraft sport fishing boat named the Rebel Yell. It had a deep V hull and two 170 horse power mercury engines. It could go 40 miles per hour on a smooth ocean.

It was just big enough to take out to the Gulf Stream in search of the big game fish that lurked in its waters. The Gulf Stream is about sixty miles off the South Carolina coast at its closest point to shore. It would usually take two to three hours to run out to those abundant fishing grounds on a calm day. Once there, we would fish for king mackerel, wahoo, dolphin, sailfish, tuna, and last, but most spectacular, the greatest of all sport fish, the great blue marlin.

This was quite an exciting way to spend a weekend and we had become pretty good at it. The Rebel Yell boated several four hundred pound blue marlin. We even managed to win a fishing contest or two. Many times we caught sailfish that were tagged and released. Only the ones large enough to win a contest would be brought back to shore, usually along with some good eating blue water fish. My favorite was wahoo. It sure tasted good right off the grill.

Sometimes we had to use a Louisville Slugger baseball bat that we kept on board to keep the sharks away while we tried to boat a large game fish. I have, since that time, met bigger, meaner and more aggressive sharks in the business world. Unfortunately you aren't allowed to use the Louisville Slugger to ward them off. Besides, I don't think you can cut down trees to make wooden bats anymore.

At night we would go into the little village of Garden City to the Clipper Ship seafood restaurant for dinner and drinks. The owner liked for us to provide the nightly entertainment. He encouraged us to put on a show each weekend during the summer. Willo would pull out his banjo and I would grab my guitar. We would play for the boating and fishing crowd from Murrel's Inlet until the wee hours of the morning. On rare occasions, you could even spot the most famous resident of Murrel's Inlet, author Mickey Spillane. Our playing seemed to be good for the restaurant's business. We even got a few free drinks for our effort when the owner was in a good mood.

It was mostly a sing-along kind of thing. You didn't have to be great, but you did have to be entertaining, at least until later in the evening. The audience usually got pretty tipsy as we played after dinner and that was just fine with the owner of the restaurant. He sold a lot more drinks that way.

Things could get a little out of hand from time to time. I remember Willo getting really upset one night when a very drunk lady poured her scotch and water into the sound hole of his three thousand dollar Martin d-28 guitar. She stumbled up to ask us to play some rock 'n roll song. As she leaned forward to be heard over the din of the crowd, she poured her entire drink right into the guitar. Now that was a feat in and of itself. I have never seen it duplicated anywhere else and I have played a lot of music since then. That gave a new meaning to the old toast, "down the hatch."

Willo was really angry and did not see the humor in this lady's unusual accomplishment. One thing you don't do is mess with Willo's banjo or his guitar. You can mess with anything else he owns, but he will shoot you over those instruments. We were good enough friends that he let me play his Martin from time to time. It sounded good even with me playing it. It's called Martin Magic. The strings are set very high on a Martin and it's not easy to play. If you are strong enough to chord it, without breaking your fingers, then most Martins sure do produce a quality sound.

As I mentioned earlier, Ken Allen's wife, Margo had seen our weekend act in the Clipper Ship and had asked us to put on our little show for her boss, the Governor. Ken and Margo had worked hard during Jim Edwards' campaign. After Jim won, Margo had been hired as the manager of the Governor's Mansion in Columbia. She was in charge of all the state functions held there. This was going to be a formal legislative dinner, and Margo was responsible for selecting the menu and entertainment, as well as all the other details that would ensure a successful evening.

Jim Edwards, our brand new Republican Governor, was trying to show the people of South Carolina that the world wouldn't end because there wasn't a Democrat in the governor's office.

Not since the days of reconstruction had South Carolina elected a Republican to a statewide constitutional office. Jim wanted to prove that a Republican Governor could work well with the members of the South Carolina General Assembly. The Assembly was 95% Democrat. Our performance that night was to be part of that effort. Looking back on the event, what a chance Margo took by hiring us. The chances friends take to help friends!

For two nights Willo and I were to provide the entertainment for the entire South Carolina Legislature. Ironically, as things turned out, one of the things that Governor Edwards was working on was the bill that eventually created the South Carolina Coastal Council. That bill developed into a bureaucratic nightmare that was destined to become a bigger part of my life than anyone could have known at the time. It was called the 1977 Coastal Zone Management Act. Governor Edwards had vetoed the same bill the prior year. This year was different in that the bill had passed the General Assembly with a huge veto-proof majority. It was destined to become law, like it or not.

The evening was to go like this: Willo and I would eat dinner with the guests, and after dinner we would play for about forty-five minutes. Willo brought his new South Carolina bride, Noel. My two children were small, one and two years old, so my wife, Martha, stayed at home to baby sit and I went alone.

My dinner partner was a very talented and beautiful lady, Anne Finch. She was the wife of one of the Governor's top political advisers, Raymon Finch. He was away on business, so we were seated together. Anne was going to entertain the guests after Willo and I had finished our set. She would play the piano when the party moved across the street to the Governor's mansion for cocktails.

Margo had told me that prior to her marriage to Raymon, Anne had been a professional singer and pianist in Fort Lauderdale. I remember thinking, that's just great, a musically talented lady to judge our amateur performance. I was also told that she had studied at the Julliard School of Music. Things were getting worse with every revelation.

Margo said that she played the piano like Liberace and sang like Peggy Lee. I mumbled something in my native Turkey Creek dialect about having her as competition.

When Margo asked what I had said, I just thanked her for allowing me to have this opportunity to make such a big fool of myself. To add insult to injury, she then proceeded to tell me that Anne also just happened to be a judge's daughter from of all places, patrician Philadelphia. That meant she had looks, talent, money and breeding. I had a bankrupt building company, a few bluegrass songs that I didn't know very well, and Willo Collins, who wasn't nearly as pretty.

This was intimidating. I was about ready to pack it in. Who needed this kind of pressure for fifty bucks?

Anne Finch was personable and down to earth. She made me feel very comfortable and encouraged me to relax. I was surprised when she told me that her husband, Raymon, liked to play the banjo and sing country music.

I was beginning to feel a little better. She assured me that her husband's rendition of "Just a Bowl of Butter Beans" would do Ernest Tubb proud. Now, I knew that Ernest Tubb had never sung that song in his life, but it was reassuring to know that at least she knew who Ernest Tubb was.

Well, maybe this wouldn't be so bad after all. With my confidence somewhat restored, we climbed up on the two tall stools that had been provided for the occasion. With a simple "hello, I'm Dave and hello, I'm Willo", we proceeded to pick and sing our hearts out. I don't think that my voice cracked more than three or four times and Willo said that I was only off-key for the first verse or two of some of the songs.

Fortunately, or so it seemed at the time, the legislators had plenty to drink with their dinner. We did some sing-along stuff and a few of them could even carry a tune and sang with some enthusiasm. Actually, as I look back on it, I think that we did a pretty good job. They clapped their hands to the music and genuinely seemed to have a merry ole time of it. Margo didn't seem embarrassed and said she was looking forward to the next evening. I found out something about myself that night. I really enjoyed performing. It was something that I had suspected for a long time. Even the pressure of the setting was exciting in a way.

Anne Finch had insisted that we come over to the mansion to hear her play and sing. Considering how kind she had been concerning our debut, how could we refuse? Her playing was exceptional. She had entertained in night clubs in Fort Lauderdale for seventeen years. She even knew some country songs. It was mostly music by Hank Williams and other crossover kind of artists, but she did do country.

Anne had made the introduction to the Edwards. They were top quality people. The Governor said he had really enjoyed our music. He was an even better politician than I thought. Ann, his wife, was very gracious and complimentary, as well. As the old saying goes; behind every good man is a good woman.

Being a conservative Republican on most issues, and a firm backer of Jim's campaign, it was a pleasure to finally meet the Governor and his wife in person. I found out that besides enjoying our music, Jim was also an avid hunter and fisherman just like Willo and myself. He was complaining about the lack of time to indulge in much of his favorite outdoor recreation since becoming governor. We also found we had something else in common. It seems that a great, grandmother of his was a Lucas and that we were distantly related. My outlook had definitely improved since the start of the evening.

Time passed and I formed a bluegrass band. We named it Tiller's Ferry. That's the name of an old ferry crossing on Lynches River near Turkey Creek community in Lee County, South Carolina. I had grown up in Turkey Creek.

One of my ancestors had been James Tiller who owned and operated the ferry named after his family back in the 1700s. Turkey Creek is four miles on the eastern side of Lucknow, South Carolina, and for those of you who remember the Lizard Man scare of 1989, Turkey Creek is only two miles from his home in Scape Ore Swamp. That should pinpoint the location for all of my more sophisticated readers.

Tiller's Ferry was playing almost every weekend. Eventually, Tiller's Ferry even recorded two albums. Our little group was pretty original, and we had written most of our own material. Our first album immediately went asphalt on the country music charts. I believe that our second album even went styrofoam—meaning we sold over twenty-seven copies, versus only fifteen of the first! Going gold or platinum didn't look too promising.

Raymon Finch, in the meantime, had decided to run for Governor. I was delighted and liked what I had read and heard about his politics. Besides, I had almost met him once and had even had dinner with his wife. As a gentleman, I was obliged to support him, under the circumstances. One day, while in a music store buying a new set of guitar strings, I ran into his wife, Anne again. She recognized me immediately and said that she had heard about my new group. I was somewhat surprised at that, but delighted.

I asked about her new role as Candidate Finch's wife and what she thought about the prospect of becoming South Carolina's First Lady. She was excited about the campaign. It was all new to her and she said that she felt as nervous about her role as I had about my performance at the Lace House. I realized then, that it's all a matter of outlook. Any task, no matter how big or small it seems, can be intimidating to anyone the first time around. In America, it's just a matter of how big a bite you're willing to take.

Anne asked me how often my new bluegrass band performed. I told her that we were playing about two weekends a month. I didn't tell her that Aunn's Feed Stable was the fanciest place we'd played. It was larger than a telephone booth, but not by much. At least the patrons were enthusiastic about our music. We even got a great deli sandwich between sets as payment for performing. We were attracting good crowds on the weekends and they were enjoying our music. Fred Aunn, the owner, even began to pay us for our work. Although encouraged by real money instead of cornbeef, I wasn't quite ready to give up my day job.

During my conversation with Anne, I volunteered the band to provide some entertainment for Raymon's campaign. She was delighted that we would help and gave me the campaign manager's name and telephone number. We made the call and he asked us to play for two or three functions. They even paid us pretty good money. Thank goodness they didn't call Fred Aunn to find out how cheaply we could be hired.

Just before we played for the first campaign rally, Anne invited me to meet Raymon. Martha and I went to a fund raiser at a private home where Anne made the introductions. What a charmer Raymon turned out to be that night. Tall and articulate, he was certainly impressive. We liked him immediately. He enjoyed playing the banjo, so he had to be a good guy, right? Other people liked him too. The campaign was going well. I had heard a great deal about him through the years. He is a redhead with a classic redhead's temperament. Brilliant, shrewd and talented, Raymon was destined to be our next governor--or so I thought.

Raymon should have followed Jim Edwards into the governor's mansion and he came heartbreakingly close to winning the nomination, but fell short by a few hundred votes. In retrospect, I suppose there are numerous reasons for his defeat. I'll never know all of them. Perhaps the biggest factor had to do with timing. His opponent for the Republican nomination was a popular pecan farmer who had been a congressman from the fifth district of South Carolina and, therefore, already had a political organization in place. Raymon didn't have good statewide name recognition. His opponent did. Raymon had started his campaign from way behind. In the last few days of the race, he had almost closed the gap. But, as we all know, *close* only counts in hand grenades and horseshoes. Raymon's campaign just plain ran out of time. Another week and I believe that he would have won pulling away.

I had only known him for a short time, and under very specific circumstances at that. The more time I spent around Raymon, the more impressed I was with him. But, I was to understand much more about the man over the next few years.

My real education was about to begin. It was to be an intense learning experience.

Looking back, I am amazed at the accuracy of his political intuition. He would make the most astounding and sometimes seemingly outrageous political predictions. At the time, I would think that he was being overly dramatic, or too flamboyant. Some of his statements seemed wildly off-base. But he predicted, years in advance, such things as the size of the soaring government deficits, the savings and loan scandal, the crash of the real estate market, the threat to the constitution posed by the seemingly innocent environmental movement, and the rise of Wall Street's prosperity at the expense of other areas of the economy, i.e., the real estate industry.

In addition, he predicted by name, the rise to political power of a knight on a white horse charging in to save us all from our own folly. This knight would be a man with a strong individual personality and would appear on the scene when things really seemed hopeless to tell the people that he could save their economic well-being by implementing strong and seemingly radical solutions to national problems.

In 1985, he said that the list of potential white knight presidential contenders would include perhaps one of the following people: Lee Iacocca, Donald Trump, or Ross Perot. At the time, I thought he wasn't serious and dismissed his pre-diction, but the 1992 Presidential election fea-tured candidate Ross Perot with just such a strong and bold campaign theme. But, I am getting ahead of my story.

Getting back to 1978, Raymon, for a combina-tion of reasons lost the primary election. Shortly after that, he and Anne moved to the Isle of Palms, just outside beautiful and historic Charleston, South Carolina. There, Raymon and his broth-ers, Henry and Mike, owned and operated a suc-cessful barrier island real estate development company and world class destination resort. Back then, it was known as the Isle of Palms Beach and Racquet Club, later renamed Wild Dunes.

It was December, 1978, by this time, and my business fortunes were heading nowhere fast. I was a young, struggling, single family homebuilder, with a wife and two young children trying my best to build a business with absolutely no capital. That was tough enough to do in a good economy, but when you added in the high inter-est rates that were prevalent in the late 1970s and early 1980s, I could see that the immediate future didn't look too promising. I was experienc-ing the stagflation of the Carter years up close and personal. Stagflation and high interest rates were winning and I was not.

Luckily for me, Raymon needed a custom

homebuilder to complete the team that he was assembling to develop the Beach and Racquet Club. I made myself available and let Raymon know that I was interested in participating in more than just his political campaigning. I told him that I was a good residential contractor, as well as a great bluegrass picker. Then, of course, I made my pitch to build houses for his company at the Beach and Racquet Club. I was soon asked to meet with Raymon and his brothers.

They evidently liked what they saw. I was offered the job of heading up a custom home building company for their partnership at the Beach and Racquet Club. I accepted, and with great expectations for the future, moved to the Isle of Palms in February of 1979. My wife, Martha, and the children moved down in the summer of that same year after we sold our home in Columbia.

Life on the island was very different from what I was used to back in Columbia and Turkey Creek. In Columbia, we lived in typical suburbia USA. The homes there were very nice, but modest. We lived in houses that I had built for sale, but for which I had not yet found a buyer. I believe we lived in four different houses during the first three years of our marriage. My wife Martha had become quite the professional mover.

My boyhood home in Turkey Creek, S.C., was a small, brick house with three bedrooms and one bath. It had 900 square feet and cost 10,000 dollars to build in 1958. It was financed through the Veterans Administration. My father was a Marine Corps veteran and had seen World War II up close and personal. He had served in the jungles of Guadalcanal with the First Marine Division. He didn't talk about the war a lot, but other people had told us that he had won some decorations for bravery. His combat career ended when he came down with malaria right after his tour of duty on Guadalcanal. He spent the rest of the war on recruiting duty back in the states.

We had no air conditioning growing up in that little red brick house. In the summertime, it got hot and sticky with no place to hide! A window fan was a big luxury for us. You just had to learn to live with the heat. I was definitely not used to luxurious living conditions.

My compensation at the Beach and Racquet Club was to be a small salary, ten percent of the stock in the building company, a bonus based on profit, and I would be provided with living accommodations. So Raymon moved us into a beach house directly behind his oceanfront home. This was a nicer, more expensive home than I had ever imagined living in. Not only was it beautiful, it was right on the beach. This was too much to ask.

It didn't last long. We moved into a smaller home later that year, but I had had a taste of the good life. I was hoping that my luck was changing for the better and I rededicated myself then and there to seizing the American dream. I was going to work hard, do a good job for Raymon, and take advantage of the opportunity that he had given me.

The next few months saw the resort business booming.

Things were going well with the new company and I was performing successfully in my role as contractor/developer. This was certainly a different setup for me professionally. I was not used to being involved with a company that was properly capitalized. I soon realized that it was not only the Finch family that was involved with the Beach and Racquet Club, but also two of the most successful and respected family business groups in the state.

The first group was headed by Wilbur Smith. Mr. Wilbur Smith had built one of the largest and most successful engineering firms in the world, Wilbur Smith and Associates. They were traffic experts. Mr. Wilbur, as he was known to people in South Carolina, traveled over 300,000 air miles a year, and was in his mid-seventies. He was always returning from such exotic places as Hong Kong, Singapore, Beijing, Paris, London, Moscow, Cairo, and Casablanca. I was impressed with that lifestyle. My major at the University of South

Carolina had been International Relations and this world traveling stuff was right up my alley.

The J.C. Long family was the other major partner. In fact, the Finch family had purchased the property directly from J.C. Long in 1972. He was reputed to be one of the most successful real estate developers in the entire Southeast. The rumor was that his businesses at one time paid over ten per-cent of the property taxes for Charleston County. I bet that was one hellacious tax bill to pay each year.

Life was good on the Isle of Palms. I was no longer just a small time developer/builder/contractor, chronically under capitalized, destined to struggle for a living all of my life. My father had worked for thirty years as an instrument mechanic at the DuPont Synthetic cloth plant in Camden, South Carolina. It was a good living, but the opportunities were limited there. My grandfather had been a small farmer and was financially devastated by the great depression of the 1930s. Now I was the president of a successful well-funded company with an unlimited future. I felt that anything was possible, and I was determined to give it my best shot. After all, my board of directors certainly could teach me about success. It was an opportunity not to be taken lightly.

My father liked to remind me that it only happened because James Farmer, a tenant farmer in Turkey Creek had taught my father to play the guitar back in the 1930s. Little did my Daddy, the late W.D. Lucas realize, that when he and my Uncle Darby Lucas were teaching me to play the guitar and sing, they were preparing me for success, not in the music field, but in the business world. I sure am glad Raymon liked the banjo and country music.

As 1979 rolled on, the Presidential campaign began to heat up. There was a host of candidates vying to become the Republican nominee. President Jimmy Carter was having one hell of a time directing Americas' fortunes. He seemed vulnerable and a lot of people wanted to take his place as leader of the free world. It seemed that he was destined to become a one-term President. Raymon's political juices were flowing again and the talk of presidential politics was heating up in South Carolina.

Raymon and I both liked what Ronald Reagan had to say. I had followed his career from his Hollywood days and respected him and his ideas. After being elected as governor of California, his political star was shining bright and he was my choice. When he ran for president the first time, I was very disappointed by his defeat. I believed that he stood for the best things about America and that he would be able to reverse the growth of big government in Washington.

Raymon felt the same way. I was really excited when Raymon became the Reagan campaign's financial director for South Carolina. That gave me the opportunity to become involved more closely in a presidential campaign, and this time around I would be able to really contribute something besides personal support. Now, I could do more than just talk and vote. Much of my time was spent in the Reagan state campaign organization as an aid to Raymon. I began helping Raymon in his role as Reagan's chief fund raiser, and we traveled the state from one end to the other as Raymon made speech after speech. He spent endless hours on the telephone trying to raise funds and I would help return calls. As I drove Raymon from place to place, he would practice his speeches and ask for my comments. I was usually pretty honest and that, more often than not, resulted in a good ass chewing. But it was worth every blister that he raised on my rear end. Raymon was very successful in his role as state finance director and surrogate speaker.

This was not an easy job, especially looking back from today's vantage point. Reagan had stumbled early and lost some of his first primaries. He was also considered by the mainline national press to be a radical and, therefore, dangerous conservative. This press bias, along with the early primary losses had brought out doubt in a lot of people's minds. But Raymon and our group of dedicated Reaganites pressed on determinedly. We were true believers in that 1980s Reagan message. We still are. Unfortunately for us and the country, something happened on the way to the Reagan Revolution. A lot of it got lost and never arrived. The components that did arrive turned out to be a little different than we expected.

At the time of this primary, the main Republican power structure in South Carolina was supporting Governor John Connally of Texas. We had some very tough adversaries allied against us and the going was not easy or the outcome secure. Both Governor Jim Edwards and U.S. Senator Strom Thurmond were against us in the primary. In South Carolina Republican politics, that was a very strong group of popularly elected officials. They don't get any better in politics than Senator Strom Thurmond and his staff.

We did have a bright group of young "up and comers" with us that proved to be a winning combination. The most well known of our group of politicians were two rising stars. The head of the campaign was Congressman Carol Campbell from Greenville. Along with Carol was an old friend of mine that I had worked with briefly during the 1968 Nixon campaign. He was a young guy named Atwater, Lee Atwater. Lee was already well-known in South Carolina political circles as a political strategist. In the not so distant future, he was to become famous in national political circles as well.

We also had the backing of the Young Republicans' organization. Linda Wilson Reed was our organizer and contact with that group. South Carolina's Young Republicans had become very influential within Republican politics on both the state and national level. Atwater had orchestrated and Finch had funded the campaign of David Barron to become president of the national organization of Young Republicans. When he was elected, Linda was able to use the manpower generated by that campaign for the most important job of canvassing, polling, and finally getting out the vote for Ronald Reagan.

With extremely hard work, dedication, great planning and of course, the best candidate, we helped win South Carolina's Republican primary for Ronald Reagan. This was his first primary victory in the south and from then on the momentum that he gained grew. It was exciting to be a part of that historical primary process. We were proud of bringing this bell weather southern state into the Reagan column. Our group was even prouder of the fact that the political odds were stacked against us. Of course, Ronald Reagan went on to win many more primary victories and eventually became the Republican candidate for President. Jim Edwards and Strom Thurmond got on board with lots of enthusiasm.

In November, he was swept into office with an electoral college landslide.

I had come a long way. My first political activism was way back in 1964. I had started out by selling cans of ginger ale door to door in my little hometown to raise money for Barry Goldwater. It was a pretty good gimmick. Goldwater for Goldwater. It worked, too—at least in South Carolina. We sold a good many cans of that stuff. This time around, I was much more involved than selling cans of ginger ale for a quarter. We were selling Doctor Ronald Reagan's True Government Limiting Elixor. It was going to cure bloated government-caused ills and help stop that out-of-control growth feeling the central government was giving to its citizens. This sure had been a lot more fun than simply watching the election process on television. We had won the Presidential battle and I had helped. Life was good and it was about to get even better.

Our Governor, Jim Edwards, was appointed Secretary of Energy in Reagan's first cabinet. Jim asked Raymon to be on his transition team. Business at the Beach and Racquet Club was good, so Raymon felt that he could accept the challenge. We sent him off to Washington with high hopes. Looking back now, this was a decisive step in the evolution of my life. The things that Raymon saw and heard during this period in Washington, D.C., were to influence his decisions regarding the political future of the country and consequently what was going to happen to the real estate industry. His financial future, after all, was tied to the real estate industry in a big way.

After arriving in Washington, Raymon became concerned over the way the new administration was shaping up. Raymon was becoming increasingly concerned with the changes in direction of the Reagan Revolution. In fact, he harangued all those in the administration who would listen that their unbalanced fiscal policies would result in accumulating a monstrous national debt. The conservatism of the power elite around the President apparently didn't extend to fiscal matters.

Not much attention was given to this fact at the time by most of the people who had supported the Reagan Revolution. There were some voices crying in the wilderness; way, way, way out in the wilderness. No one heard the warning.

Looking back, how can you expect to cut the power of government by tremendously increasing the amount of money it spends? The world doesn't work that way. Money is power and as long as the money flows to Washington, the power will flow in direct proportion. The more money the government gets, the more power it will buy and *use*.

There were other more exciting and controversial social and international issues that got priority. The President's attention went to other areas and the growing federal deficit was about to explode. I can still remember my feelings of shock and dismay when I saw that first Reagan Budget. I could not believe what I was seeing. But there it was. Instead of a reduction in spending, this budget called for a huge increase.

Raymon and his boss, Jim Edwards, had opposed the huge increases in the budget. The more they spoke out against the big spending plans, the more unwelcome they were in the inner circle of the administration. The few fiscal conservatives that were in the administration had only two choices: either keep quiet and go along to get along, and stay in the game, or, they could resign. Jim Edwards, to his eternal credit, resigned.

The big spenders won out and what happened next is history. The interest of the big banks, big business, and Wall Street won out over main street America. The small business man, the small farmer, the little guy who believed in the Reagan Revolution and made it possible, never knew what hit them. What was good for Wall Street, corporate America, and the big banks was suddenly the only thing that was really good for America.

There is some truth in that philosophy. In the short run, it was certainly better than the alternative, which was the destruction of our traditional American values. But no one group holds the key to the future. America was founded by both the large and the small man, both the successful and the unsuccessful. Thomas Paine didn't win any Harvard Business School achievement awards, but he was just as important to this country as the very wealthy and successful George Washington or Ben Franklin.

Big debt needed big lenders. And boy, did we ever get big debt. We had been hoping for a large decrease in the budget. This would have forced the Democrats to push for spending increases and the battle for the future direction of our country could have been won then and there. Instead, we got the largest increase in debt in the history of the world. I think that I understand the dynamics involved. The Republicans wanted a bigger military, the Democrats wanted bigger social programs and what we got was a sellout from both sides. They gave us the debt that is now eating away at America's future.

There were, of course, trade offs that came from such large amounts of spending. The big banks had gotten themselves into trouble by lending money to an assortment of third world countries. Most of those loans became deeply troubled loans. This money should have been put to use here in America to begin with. The huge increase in borrowing by the federal government allowed the banks to absorb the hit from those bad debts and to regain financial stability. The huge spending increases were an indirect way to bail out the banking system. It was a neat little trick and it worked. But, with the increased flow of money to the government, came an increase in its power, and in my opinion, this increase in power is the major danger to our cherished American freedoms.

I have relayed this story only to set the stage for what happened over the next three years. When Raymon returned from Washington, he was convinced that due to the budget deficits, our economy was in for a rough, long-term future. He felt that by 1986 or 1987 the real estate values of the country would be in a tail spin. There, of course, were many other factors involved in Raymon's thinking during this period. Another event that had really gotten his attention, happened right in our own back yard. Green politics, no growth policies, and the drawbridge mentality had now taken over the local government. A no growth, little old lady in tennis shoes, with a "not in my backyard" group took over city hall. She had been elected our new mayor on the Isle of Palms and immediately, the atmosphere on the island changed.

The Beach and Racquet Club had once been a welcomed addition to island life, but was now despised by the new people in power. The islanders split into two groups; those who were for development, and those who were against anything that anyone wanted to do to expand growth on the Isle Of Palms. The "moat around my home crowd" was now in charge.

This was the last straw for Raymon. He convinced his other partners that they should get out of the resort business while the getting was good. The idea to sell the newly renamed Wild Dunes Resort was formalized by the board of directors in the spring of 1983. It was kept graveyard quiet. No outside real estate brokers were allowed to know that Wild Dunes was on the market. This was to be done as quickly and silently as possible.

We began to see exotic people showing up and being entertained by Raymon and Anne. There were rich Arabs, wealthy Latino's, sophisticated Europeans, and even some very famous American businessmen that came to look and dicker.

Raymon was a tough customer in politics and an even tougher customer when it came to his business. He is the consummate entrepreneur. A C.P.A. by training and profession, Raymon had been the Partner in Charge of the state of South Carolina for the largest international accounting firm in the world. With his background in tax matters, Governor Edwards appointed Raymon to the South Carolina Tax Commission.

He was successful in many types of business ventures. Comfortable with emerging technologies, one of his earliest profitable ventures had been in the computer services industry.

He had a price in mind and was not about to sell his creation to just anyone. He was determined to find a suitable buyer who could carry on his vision for Wild Dunes. So 1983 seemed to be the year that my new found prosperity would end. My future hung in the balance. What was I to do?

My company was not part of the transaction. It looked like I would soon be in business for myself with not much capital once again. Suddenly an idea popped into my brain. This was America, the land of opportunity. Was it possible that I could purchase Wild Dunes? How could I possibly come up with the fifty million dollar sales price? What I needed was a way to borrow big money fast. How's a thing like that work, anyway?

The beachfront looking east at Wild Dunes.

2

Who Me?!

OR:

**How Ronald Reagan Rewarded
Me for My Faith**

As 1983 drew to a close, it became apparent
that the sale of Wild Dunes was going to take
place. It was just a matter of time. I had been
asking Raymon to sell a parcel of oceanfront land
to me so that I could build a high-end condominium project. The land was situated on the 18th
green of the now, world famous Wild Dunes Links
Golf Course. Raymon had wanted the partnership to develop this oceanfront property, but the
other partners didn't want to risk going any further into debt. Raymon and the board had little
faith that I could get the money to build this
project, but as a favor they had agreed to give me
the opportunity to try.

So in the fall of 1983 I negotiated an option to purchase the oceanfront parcel that surrounds and overlooks the 18th green of the 34th best golf course in the world. I was not required to put up much earnest money, and the partnership granted me six months to get the deal done. I had to get an architect to design the project, price the project, find the right lender, and close the whole deal within a short six months. All I needed was ten million dollars cash at closing. No terms were given. The board wanted just cash and a lot of it. I didn't think about the difficulty of trying to do this deal; I only thought about the end result. I had nothing to lose and everything to gain. After all, this was America, the land of opportunity.

I had been taught that hard work, honesty, and a little luck could make your fortune. My work days stretched into eighteen to twenty hour marathons. I looked around for help with the financing and found it in an old college buddy, Hank Holiday, who was now working for Bank of America in Atlanta, Georgia. Hank and I had known each other at the University of South Carolina in Columbia during our undergraduate days, the late 1960s. He had gone into the mortgage brokerage business and had become quite successful. I think that he was even the top national producer for BA at the time. We were reacquainted by an old mutual friend, Jerry Scurry. Jerry had grown up in Columbia but had recently moved to Charleston. Scurry and I had worked together as real estate brokers in Columbia. Jerry came from an old Columbia family that went back many generations in that city. Raymon was also originally from Columbia and Jerry had known him for a long time. He had brokered some real estate for Raymon in the past and they had become friends.

Jerry was trying to broker tracts of land for Raymon at Wild Dunes and I was constantly trying to figure out how to get my deals done before someone like him sold the deals out from under me. He had successfully brokered some oceanfront land to a competing developer the year before. That project was close to selling out and the guy wanted to purchase more land in Wild Dunes. So I got Jerry to work with me instead of against me and that killed two birds with one stone.

At Jerry's invitation, Hank came to Wild Dunes and promptly fell in love with the place. It's a very beautiful and captivating island. I presented my deal to him and he was excited about becoming a part of the development team. We polished up my package and began to put the dog and pony show together for the national lending market.

This was Hank's strong point. He really knew how to put a real estate package together to attract the big national lenders. We targeted a limited number to approach with our package. These were lenders that Hank either knew from past deals, or from telephone inquiries. He felt that perhaps they would be interested in our kind of deal. After a few presentations, it became apparent that the timing was excellent and that quite a few lenders were interested. This was getting exciting.

One group in particular showed a lot of enthusiasm. They were from Rochester, N.Y. The institution was the Rochester Community Savings Bank. Hank and I took their representatives out on the golf course one windswept November day. We walked up on the 18th green and stood on the sand dunes that surround that hole. The view was spectacular. It was the kind of sight that really gets the daydreams flowing. I believe that it was just after lunch around two p.m. It was one of those warm autumn days with crystal blue skies and white sandy beaches gleaming in the Carolina sun. The sea grass was waving in the soft breeze and the sea gulls were sailing over head yelling out their shrill cries. From the north came line after line of brown pelicans on their way to winter away from the harsh northern cold that had already gotten its grip on the Rochester area.

Hank and I started to paint beautiful pictures of our condominium proposal for our guests. We had an artist's rendering of the proposed project with us. The artist and the architect had both conjured up a great looking project. The lenders from Rochester seemed to like what they were seeing and hearing. It is sometimes easier to sell the sizzle than the steak. That day we had plenty of sizzle to sell. And at least in this instance, the steak was better than the sizzle.

Everybody has his own private dreams of what life would be like living in such romantic circumstances. Picture in your mind the romantic old south of the Charleston low country. Then, feel the soft southern sea breezes as they press softly against your face. You're standing on your balcony overlooking the bright blue sea and the spectacular 18th green of the world renowned Wild Dunes Links Course. (Now, wipe the seaspray from your eyes and read on.)

We must have said the right things that day because we got a verbal commitment for $10,000,000 right on the spot. The next few weeks we worked out the details and brought in the Bank of America to provide construction financing for our condo project, as well. In the meantime, Raymon had been stepping up his campaign to sell the entire resort; development property, golf course, tennis courts, rental sales company, restaurants, conference facilities, retail sales department, in short, the whole kit and kaboodle.

I had learned through my conversations with Raymon that the price had been lowered somewhat.

They had almost sold Wild Dunes to an Arab investor. The contracts had been prepared and almost signed, but at the last minute the buyers backed out. I understood that there were even serious discussions with a Dallas, Texas family that was reputed to be richer than chocolate cake. They were pretty tough businessmen, however, and their offer was too low to accept.

It was January of 1984 and I had several lenders eager to participate in this booming resort project of mine. Raymon was about to start the long process of locating another potential buyer, after refusing the last offer. Buyers for this kind of deal were few and hard to find.

That's when it dawned on me. If I could raise ten million dollars cash for a small parcel of land, why not go after the whole thing? But did I dare go after something this big? I already had in my possession a commitment for a big chunk of the asking sales price. Could I find a lender to put up the rest? If I had been able to convince people to loan large sums of money for just one parcel of land, then perhaps my team could convince them to loan enough to buy the entire resort.

I talked to Hank. At first he was hesitant and thought that it wouldn't work because my financial statement was too small. I told him that if they would lend me ten million dollars on that same weak financial statement, then it must be the value of the land and not my financial statement that was paramount. That argument seemed to convince him. After looking at the numbers, he agreed that it might work.

He made a few calls to some additional lenders. After getting their reaction he became more convinced than ever that I was right and that it might be possible. He cautioned that it would be a difficult thing to accomplish and reminded me that we were competing with sophisticated businessmen who had very strong financial statements. The Arab couple that had almost bought Wild Dunes earlier, was from a very influential royal Middle Eastern family. You don't find many financial statements stronger than theirs.

The first hurdle was to convince Raymon and his partners that I could produce when others with much more experience, money, and better banking connections had failed. This wouldn't be easy since some of Raymon's partners were also interested in buying the property. The numbers were large, but the arithmetic was simple. The cash needed to purchase the entire island resort was $25,000,000. Then, there would be an assumption of existing debt, and additional outside funding to complete the amenity package. I had already found $10,000,000—a big portion of the $25,000,000 total cash needed. It was time now to convince Raymon that I could find the rest of the money before one of the other potential buyers got serious.

I knew that Raymon wanted to give me the opportunity, but until that commitment for $10,000,000 came through from the Rochester Bank, I hadn't the credibility needed for him to convince his partners. Raymon was tough to deal with, and did not want to show any favoritism. He had always been tougher on me than anyone else who worked there, but then he expected more from me. The other partners didn't want to waste time on me when they could be spending time finding a real buyer.

Raymon had a difficult time with them, but the fact that there were no strong buyers just at that moment opened the door for him. It was just a tiny crack of an opening, but it proved to be just enough. The $10,000,000 commitment finally came through in writing and convinced Raymon that I was capable of producing. The same argument that I had used on Hank seemed to work well. It also frightened some of the other partners that were thinking of buying the place themselves.

After several weeks of negotiations, I signed an option agreement to purchase the whole of Wild Dunes. The price was reasonable. The business was good. Lenders were interested and I was acceptable to them as a developer. God, I loved the 1980s. All Reaganomics weren't bad, contrary to today's political correctness and my earlier comments.

But, there was a major problem. We signed the option on February the 3rd. The option had given me only until March the first to not only find the money required, (a big job in itself) but to close the transaction. To close a fifty million dollar real estate deal takes time under the best of conditions. Just the legal work and the documentation, under normal circumstances, would take weeks or months to prepare. There were several different corporations and partnerships involved in the ownership of Wild Dunes. Each officer and partner of each entity had to sign separate documents. All of the titles had to be researched and then the proper documents had to be drawn up.

Even more daunting, an appraisal of all the different parcels of land involved would be required before any lender would give us an answer. This was an immense and time consuming undertaking in itself. All of this had to occur at the same time that we were trying to find the rest of the money or there wouldn't be enough time to get it done. It all had to take place within four weeks. And, in addition to these time problems, I had no money.

I had to find accountants, lawyers, and appraisers to work on the come. They had to agree that the only way to get paid was to close the deal. If the deal didn't close they had worked for free.

Each one of them had to be acceptable to the financial institutions that became involved, so I couldn't use just anyone. If you have ever been through the experience of buying a house, then you know at least some of the problems that we faced. The only good thing was that 1984 was a leap year and we had an extra day to get it done.

No one thought that I could do it within the time frame that I was given. But that was what they thought. Once the option was signed, I put my team to work. First, Hank lined up a first class appraiser—one of the best in the business-—Mr. Don Pardue. Don was out of Atlanta, Georgia, and came with the highest credentials. His appraisals were accepted by all of the major financial institutions in the southeast.

It took some doing, but Hank and I convinced Don to drop everything else and concentrate exclusively on our project. He also agreed to do it with only a small retainer.

Next we found two young attorneys, Foster Gaillard and Henry Fishburne to do the legal work. They agreed to a contingency arrangement. They would only get paid if we were successful in putting our deal together. Their entire firm would have to spend four weeks nonstop working on this deal. They were gambling that it would close.

Next, Hank introduced me to a Charleston tax and real estate attorney. He would also function as the accountant. He had helped put some of Hank's other deals together. He also agreed to work "on the come." With this team in place, and the option in hand, we went to work. Hank and I put the new package together with the help of all the others involved.

Pardue literally moved to Charleston and had preliminary numbers for us within a week. Don needed backup information, but at least we had a realistic preliminary range of value to work with. Don's educated estimate was that the deal would appraise for over $100,000,000. If this were true, this made our loan to value ratio around 50 percent. It was extremely good news.

As Don's backup research came in, that ratio eventually dropped to less than 33 percent or one third of the purchase price. This was beginning to look like a very good real estate buy. Of course, this value would only be realized from sales over a number of years.

To reach this goal would take a period of 10 to 15 years. Hank and I eventually presented our package to ten interested financial institutions. All of them came to Wild Dunes to look at the investment, and all of them indicated that they were interested.

However, time was very short, so we didn't have the luxury of a long courtship. We had a wedding date and needed a bride. The days flew by.

The last week approached and although there was a lot of interest, there was still no commitment. We had done all that we could do except wait. Then the phone rang. A Texas savings and loan offered a 50/50 joint venture. We asked them to put it in writing and then sat by the telex machine. This was pre-facsimile machine days and things took a little longer. Finally it came.

The excitement grew. We now officially had the money. If we could bring everything together, this was going to work. A few days before this good news, Hank and I had approached a Florida institution called Sunrise Savings and Loan. We had flown to their home office located in Boyenton Beach, Florida. There, we made a very good presentation to their loan committee.

They liked the deal and offered to send their entire board of directors up to the Isle of Palms to see the property so they could make a quick decision. This was the only way that they could possibly meet our time frame. They were true to their word, and their board of directors had left the resort in a good frame of mind. Over dinner they had truly seemed impressed with the opportunity. It didn't hurt that we were able to show them the letter from the "Texicans." A little competition can be very helpful.

The Texas boys began to press us for an answer. They had given us a twenty-four hour dead-

line to accept their offer and time was quickly
running out. The way things were shaping up,
the Sunrise deal was by far the best, but as yet
there was no word. We were on the verge of accepting the Texas offer. We debated and an-
guished over what to do. Finally the call from
Sunrise came through. They didn't want to be a
joint venture partner. They would make us a
straight loan with the land and businesses as col-
lateral. The $10,000,000 that had been commit-
ted from the Bank of America and Rochester
Savings Bank could be used as the equity needed
to make the deal for Wild Dunes go through.

The cost of the transaction was high, but not
prohibitively so. The interest rates quoted were
market rates. This seemed like a dream come
true. We held our breath until we received the
written commitment. It began to come over the
teletype. What if they changed something? What
would happen when the lawyers put their legalese
in? Would it still work?

The team that I had assembled poured over
the documents. The written document was something that we could live with. A huge sigh of relief was in order. The terms were workable and
after we had satisfied ourselves that this was a
good commitment, we dropped Texas and took
Florida. This way we would own 100 percent of
the deal. Sorry, Texas, but business is business.

I had gotten to know Holiday all over again during these pressure packed few weeks. I had told Hank that I would make him a full partner if he could help me pull off this deal. We had nothing in writing, just a gentleman's understanding. The two of us had agreed to reward the tax attorney with a minority position, if we were successful. This way I had these guys working very hard to do this deal for no fees up front. Since I didn't have enough money to pay their usual fees, this was the only way of getting the deal done within the required time frame.

We now had all of the necessary money committed to close the deal. I spent the days left on the option driving, not just pushing the attorneys, accountants, and the appraiser. This was going to be complicated. There were hundreds of details that had to be worked out. We had to coordinate five banks, eighteen attorneys working for the banks, five attorneys working for us, two attorneys working for Raymon, various land title attorneys, and several CPAs representing the different parties.

There were lawyers, lawyers everywhere, enough to drive me to drink (hopefully in celebration). As March 1, 1984 approached, everybody's nerves were on edge. Each lawyer had to say something about, or object to, each document's particular language. They had to justify being there and justify, more importantly, their fees. It seemed as though there was a crisis for every minute left in the contract. I had to get tough with this group or the deal wasn't going to close. There were complaints from every group involved, including my own lawyers. Several times I had to take them out behind the woodshed for a "Come to Jesus" meeting.

The closing day came and we had most of the problems ironed out. It was a long day. But, finally the time came to transfer title and pass out the checks. Without much more difficulty, it closed in time for all of the documents to be recorded at the courthouse and the checks to be deposited in each partner's bank account. The largest real estate deal in the history of the State of South Carolina had been completed. I was now the owner of one of the crown jewels of oceanfront resorts on the east coast. This was a world class property and it now belonged to me. True to my word, I admitted Hank Holiday into the partnership about three weeks after the closing.

The partnership was known as Wild Dunes Associates. I retained a 40-percent interest, Hank received a 40-percent interest, and the tax lawyer and accountant got the remaining 20-percent interest for their efforts. Rochester Community Savings Bank was now making noises about buying into the partnership. Retail real estate sales had really taken off with the news of our purchase of the resort. There had been a lot of free publicity from the surprise purchase of the property by our group of unknown players. There was much enthusiasm now, particularly from the financial institutions that had not participated in the transaction but had wanted to do the deal. They made purchase money mortgages plentiful for our buyers. This helped to move sales along at a brisk clip.

Rochester made us a very good offer. The New York bank's proposal was too good to refuse. They were admitted as 50 percent partners. The original partners had cashed in on a portion of the Wild Dunes transaction and put some money in their bank accounts. This was a dramatic change in fortune for me and the other partners.

We no longer controlled the deal, but we had been generously compensated for our loss of total ownership. The local banks had been caught napping and were a little embarrassed that out-of-state banks had command. Those same out-of-state banks now also dominated the Wild Dunes real estate lending market that the local banks at one time controlled.

Competition is a wonderful thing. All of a sudden, the local bankers made new money available for expansion and development. Other developers started to make offers on parcels of property. We had announced that our Marina was to expand from 150 boat slips to 400 slips. Construction on the second, world class golf course was started. The economy was expanding and sales really took off. Our total sales went from $33,000,000 to

$64,000,000 the first year. I was negotiating with major hotel chains to bring in a first class conference hotel. Business was going very well.

But problems within the partnership soon developed. I wanted to limit the number of units sold each year. I felt that this way our property values would be protected. After all, in business, supply and demand rule everything and I thought that we were allowing too much product to flood the market. Too much supply, and prices and demand would go down. We had cash offers from other developers that were difficult to ignore. I was the only partner who did not want to accept some of these cash proposals. Everybody else was interested in as many sales, as quickly as possible, for as much money as possible.

This was great short-term strategy, but disastrous for the future. Tensions grew between us. Then I heard about the proposed 1986 Tax Reform Act. I started going to Washington to lobby against this legislation. Congressman Campbell and my friend, Lee Atwater, told me the bill was going to pass. Although they also felt it was a bad law, this was the way the political wind was blowing. The only thing that we could do was try to retain second home mortgage interest deductions.

Even saving mortgage interest deductions on first homes was going to be a close call. And so, in 1986, the government once again changed the rules on

Oceanfront homes at Wild Dunes.

American business. Raymon had been correct in his forecast. The bill was going to be a disaster for the real estate industry and the savings and loan industry, but it was going to be passed whether we liked it or not. With these two factors staring me in the face, the proposed tax changes and the differences with my partners, I decided that I would follow Raymon and get out of the Wild Dunes partnership while there was still time. Raymon had continued to do well. In the entrepreneurial tradition he had moved to Florida, acquired two cellular telephone franchises, and built a new championship golf course. Located in West Palm Beach, Emerald Dunes was Raymon's new pride and joy. Designed and built by the world renowned golf course designer, Tom Fazio, and currently operated by his son, Ray, it is truely a golf course work of art. For a great day of golf and stimulating political dialogue, this is the place to go.

After some tough negotiations, I became a limited partner and, for a price, I relinquished most of my partnership interest. The policies of the Reagan years had worked for me and against me. They had made it possible for me to become wealthy. Now, they were threatening to take it all back through this terrible piece of legislation.

By July of 1986, I was, for all practical purposes, out of the Wild Dunes partnership that I had created less than two short years before. I was proud of what had been accomplished during this exciting time in my life. My last year as the managing general partner saw total partnership sales go over the $100,000,000 mark. The Wild Dunes partnership had become the 14th largest privately owned company in the state in sales volume. Not bad for a country boy from Turkey Creek, South Carolina. There were many people to thank for that success and I hope that over the years I have thanked them all properly.

3

Satchel Paige Was Right

OR:

How I Looked Back and They Were Gaining

Life for me was extraordinary in the years of the 1980s. I was able to accomplish many of the ambitions of my youth and some things that I had only vaguely fantasized about. As I mentioned earlier, I had formed a bluegrass band called "TILLER'S FERRY." We had been performing all over the Southeast. On average, we performed a couple of nights a week and then on about half of the weekends out of the month. Even as a small child I had enjoyed entertaining. I had inherited more than my share of "ham." Our band had gained a local following during the early 1980s. When Bob Hope came to Columbia to help Strom Thurmond with his reelection campaign, we were part of the show. Lee Atwater was now Strom Thurmond's campaign manager, and invited us to be on the program. We played at Township Auditorium in front of 5,000 fans. It was surprising that so many people came to hear us, but they really seemed to enjoy our music. Of course, Mr. Hope drew a few people on his own, I'm sure.

I was concerned that Bob Hope would have a hard time following our act, but with the help of Senator Thurmond he did just fine. We even traded jokes backstage. His jokes were as funny offstage as they were onstage. I guess that he forgot my jokes, since he didn't use them in his part of the show. That same campaign season, we gave equal time to the Democratic candidates. We even played for one of President Carter's campaign stops in South Carolina (our base player was a Democrat and demanded equal representation) as well as playing for his challenger and my candidate, Ronald Reagan. Those kind of jobs paid well; in money as well as special memories.

We played a lot of weekend bluegrass festivals and, in addition, we played the customary round of bars and honky tonks. But my favorite part of our musical career was the studio work that we did while cutting our two albums. It was hard work making those records, but it was an appealing experience for me.

The time came however, when a choice had to

be made. Playing bluegrass took up a lot of time. We had become about as good as we were going to be as semiprofessionals. To take the next big step meant doing it full time. Just at that juncture the opportunity to buy Wild Dunes came along. Since money and bluegrass music don't go together, I chose to continue with my business career. Even after buying Wild Dunes, I tried to keep my hand in the music for a time, but the business duties took over and I was forced to give it up. I miss it a lot, even today, and I am still grateful for the opportunities it circuitously gave me.

As mentioned in an earlier chapter, I had also been involved in national politics. My interest in politics had always been strong and I had worked as a volunteer for most of the major campaigns beginning with the Goldwater race back in high school. My association with Raymon Finch had allowed me to get pretty close to the major Republican candidates of the 1980s.

I had met John Connally and George Bush, as well as Ronald Reagan. I held conservative beliefs in most major issues such as national defense, the budget deficits, business issues, and the growth of governments (federal, state, and local). On other issues, more middle of the road to liberal ideas prevailed. That was particularly true when it came to issues of personal freedom, privacy, and economic opportunity. I had certainly benefited from access to the ladder of economic opportunity and I believed that a rising tide floats all boats, unless they are tied up to a stationary dock. A boat tied to a non-floating dock during a rising tide will tilt, flood and then sink.

The tide itself can be distorted by unusually severe storms, such as hurricanes and gales, and to those unprepared or without the necessary strength, disaster comes. A new state law was soon to hit with the force of a tempest. But that comes later in my story.

During the mid-eighties, I also had the opportunity to travel. Moreover, I needed to for business reasons. Although I had been a part of the previous management team at Wild Dunes, I had never been on the receiving end of the services that we provided for our guests. My idea of luxury in 1984 was to stay at an upscale Holiday Inn. Up until then, I couldn't afford even that too often. Now don't get me wrong, there are some fine Holiday Inns around. But we were talking about running a world class five star resort with an international, upscale clientele. I knew enough to know, that I didn't know enough to even know how much I didn't know. And that was a lot.

So I resolved to educate myself in the ways of the hotel and restaurant business. I had taken French in both high school and college and I had been told by experts that the French are the best in the world at preparing food and providing five star quality service. At least that's what I'd been told by people who said they were experts.

Armed with this tip, I bought a Berlitz language course to polish up on my practically forgotten french. Then I bought a plane ticket to Paris and Monte Carlo. In November of 1984, I was off to France. I learned a lot. It was hard and lonely work but someone had to do it, so I took up the challenge. I would return to France about every six months after studying the restaurant and hotel guides. Contrary to what I had heard about French treatment of Americans, we got along famously—especially, when they found out the reason for my visits to France. As soon as they understood that I was also in the hotel/restaurant business, they would roll out the red carpet and answer every question that I had. My knowledge of the resort business grew along with my knowledge of the French language. What fun!

We rebuilt my family home in Turkey Creek, S.C., in 1985. We kept it modest and as close to the original 1860s farm house as was practical. We did add a second story that was originally an attic. Then we rebuilt the old barn that had been torn down by my father in the 1960s. It was a combination horse barn with stalls on the outside, and office, and party/game room inside. My parents moved from the 900 square foot, veterans administration financed, brick home that was down a lane, into the newly rebuilt old home place.

We called the two houses, the new old house and the old new house. I still get confused. Of all the nice things that my new good fortune brought to me, the building of that place has given me and my entire family the most pleasure. My boyhood friend, J.D. Fountain, still lived in Turkey Creek. J.D. and I had owned horses growing up. Since he still lived in the country he had continued to enjoy riding and owned Arabian horses.

He had gotten into endurance racing and quickly learned that the only way to be competitive in that area was to ride Arabians. They were bred to run forty miles a day in the Arabian Deserts. Over long distances, no other breed can come close to keeping up with them. Arabians are also incredibly beautiful animals. The horse, in general, is a beautiful creature, but in my opinion, the Arabians dominate in beauty, intelligence and stamina.

We decided to buy Egyptian Arabians. Many people, including my family, think they are the rarest and most beautiful of them all. We really took to these animals. My wife, Martha, was really smitten, and became involved in the industry on a national level. She now serves on two governing boards: the AHRA and the Pyramid

Society. The AHRA stands for the Arabian Horse Registry of America and acts as the registration agency for all strains of the Arabian horse. The Pyramid Society promotes the Egyptian Arabian. Martha has become quite an ambassador for the breed.

I should have been satisfied with doing all of the above, but I made a serious mistake. I had been smart enough to get out of the speculative real estate development business at the right time, while business was still good and prices were high. The effects of the 1986 Tax Reform Act had not taken their toll yet. Things were going well. Then Brooks Harvey called me.

Brooks had been promoted to head up real estate sales for Wild Dunes. He was one of the main reasons for our sales success. I had instituted an off-site sales program just after buying Wild Dunes, and Brooks had been my man in charge. He did an excellent job. We decided that instead of spending 1.5 million dollars a year on advertising we could save money by sending our salesmen to the clients for much less.

Our salesman would have a client, for instance, from Cleveland who had bought property at Wild Dunes. He would ask for the names of a group of his friends, relatives, or business associates. Then we would sponsor a nice reception in Cleveland for this group of people. We would take our property to the potential buyer with slides, movies, brochures, maps, pictures, and most of all, enthusiasm from our sales staff and the client that was already a property owner with us.

All of this was done at first class locations like The Carlyle Hotel in Manhattan or the Ritz Carlton in Atlanta. It worked well. We sold a lot of property and drastically reduced our advertising budget. This was the system that allowed our sales to soar to over 100 million dollars while I was the managing general partner.

So now that I was no longer his boss or an active partner, Brooks decided that he wanted to do me a favor in return for his past promotion. Oceanfront lots were, dollar for dollar, the best investment in Wild Dunes. Over the ten years preceding 1986, they had increased in value at the rate of twenty percent a year. There were only a few lots remaining on the oceanfront. Most of the other oceanfront lots had been built on by this time. It was possible that within four to seven years you could double your money, if you bought one of the last five or six undeveloped beachfront lots in Wild Dunes.

I bit hard. I purchased lots number 11 and number 13 in the Dunesridge West subdivision. I paid $475,000 for one and $485,000 for the other. I planned to build a home for myself on number 11 and a speculative house on number 13.

I purchased the two lots and contacted Edgar Wiggins to do the architectural work for my personal home. Edgar was the first architect to move to Hilton Head Island when Charles Fraser started Sea Pines Plantation in the late 1950s,. Edgar had helped me with projects at Wild Dunes and had been a big factor in my success. I put my brother, Stephen, in charge of designing the speculative home on the other lot.

Stephen had been my right arm in the construction days at the old Beach and Racquet Club. He acted as my construction superintendent and had done one hell of a job as a contractor. He chose a local architect to design the house for lot number 13. This was in the late fall of 1986, after leaving the Wild Dunes partnership.

My wife, Martha, began work with Ed Wiggins in designing our next home. She had some definite ideas on what she wanted. I suppose that sounds familiar to most men who are married. I know that isn't a "politically correct" thing to say now, but it's true, none the less. The other design didn't take as much time. By early spring 1987, Stephen was ready to submit preliminary plans for a building permit.

The house plan was excellent and although the lot was narrow, the architect, Joe Tucker, had come up with a design that allowed for a swimming pool situated on the ocean. With only eighty feet in width to work with, I was quite impressed with the layout that he and brother Stephen had created. Stephen was ready to apply to Wild Dunes Community Association for a building permit. The permitting procedure for building a house in Wild Dunes worked as follows: First, you submitted plans to the Wild Dunes Homeowners Association. Then, they checked to see if the plans conformed to the existing covenants of the Wild Dunes Zoning Ordinance.

This document had been in place since the early 1970s, It had been approved by the local city council. Then, it had been approved by the county zoning board. After that it had passed the state regulators. Finally, it had gone through the federal registration process. A partial list of the federal agencies involved includes the Securities and Exchange Commission, the Army Corp of Engineers, the Department of Housing and Urban Development (HUD), and the Environmental Protection Agency.

I believe that the zoning for those two lots had been approved by no less than fifteen federal, state, county and local governmental bodies. All of these agencies had been given the opportunity to comment and to make sure that the planned residential development was in compliance with their Byzantine laws, rules and regulations. Of course, they all charged the developer a small fortune for the privilege of having them perform their super-fluous and redundant due diligence procedures. These costs were then passed on to the buyer of the various properties. If you wanted to build a house on one of the lots, the Wild Dunes Archi-tectural View Board would check your plans first.

After the Wild Dunes people made sure that you were in compliance with this document, they issued you a Wild Dunes building permit. This document entitled the holder to move up in the chain of aggravation, frustration, and expense. Now the supplicant could approach a real gov-ernment bureaucrat. These were the people who worked at the City of the Isle of Palms. Most of these folks were nice people to deal with when I started building on the Isle of Palms. That con-tinued to be the case until the little ole lady in tennis shoes, became the mayor of the island and began to promote her political agenda of "no one else on my island." Then things started to get dif-ficult. Even if your project conformed to all zon-ing regulations, if she didn't like it, then you would be forced into a public hearing. If the council voted against you, the only remedy was the court and that was expensive and there was no guarantee that you would win.

We will not call her by name, but will use the code name of "she who opposes all." After much nitpicking to see if you conformed to "she who opposes all's" idea of the PRD (Planned Residential Development) zoning of Wild Dunes, you were then allowed to apply for a building permit. And, of course, since the level of aggravation and frustration continued to increase, the level of expense also increased. You had to pay for another permit.

Like some real-life Nintendo game, each level was harder and more dangerous. It is also a damned sight more expensive. A permit from the South Carolina Coastal Council was required to complete the process. Each procedure must take place in the required order. You cannot get the permit from the Coastal Council without first getting a permit from the City of the Isle of Palms; and that permit would not be issued until you had one from Wild Dunes. That should have been easy for me to do. After all, I had been the managing general partner just a few months before we submitted this permit application, and I was still a partner in the Wild Dunes Associates Limited Partnership. But I guess that a bureaucrat is always a bureaucrat.

Even though the plans that we had submitted conformed to all the internal and external laws and regulations, they turned us down. The way the house was situated on the lot caused it to extend toward the ocean and out past the neighbor's house by about ten feet. The house was still not into the dunes and was even twenty-five feet short of the legal limits. Even though the plans were legal, and conformed to all rules and codes, the building permit was denied by The Wild Dunes Homeowners Association.

We requested a conference with the Home-owners Association. They admitted they knew that legally, if I pressed, they would have to give in and issue the required permit. They felt that the ten additional feet might possibly cause a problem with my new neighbors. I didn't want to rock the boat, or get off on the wrong foot with my new neighbor, so I voluntarily agreed to try and change the design of the house.

It had been several months since the purchase of the lots, and I had spent a lot of money on this project, but now it was going to take more time and more money. This is a good example of the mind set that American business operates under today. How can you do business if the rules un-der which you operate are changed at the whim of a bureaucrat? The scary part is that this bu-reaucrat worked for private enterprise. I hadn't even begun to deal with the first level of govern-ment.

Back to the drawing boards went Steve and Joe. Try as they might over the next few weeks, the lot was just too narrow to allow for everything that the market dictated we build. The cost of the lot, the design process, and the interest on the newly acquired lot mortgage was expensive. With the money and time already invested in this project, we needed to sell it for a profit soon or it was going to be a loser.

All that we had for our efforts at this point, was wasted time and wasted money. At each subsequent meeting with Steve and Joe, it became apparent that if we wanted to build for the targeted market we had to include a pool—most of the beachfront homes in the area had pools. The old design was the only thing that really fit the bill. The problem was that alternative plans would have required the pool to be built too close to the dune lines. If we changed plans to suit our neighbors, then we would be affecting more of the dune area, and would run afoul of real legal state and city ordinances. I was getting upset. Little did I know, this was just the beginning.

My own house plans were now complete. Since we weren't going to build a pool and our lot was a few feet wider than the other lot, there were no conflicts with the existing system. It was late fall of 1987 and we went ahead and put our existing house on the market. We expected it to sell in the spring of 1988 and we were going to start construction as soon as we had a good solid contract.

During this same time, I heard of the pending beachfront legislation in Columbia. I immediately asked if the legislation contained a grandfather clause. A grandfather clause would usually exempt existing projects. I was assured that it did and that my land would be one of the properties exempted from this proposed law. Reassured by this and the basic property rights secured by both my state and federal constitutions, I relaxed my guard.

That was a big mistake. The bill passed and was signed into law in the summer of 1988. The regulations that were put out by the Coastal Council gutted the grandfather language in the bill. It only grandfathered property that had been issued a building permit within a certain amount of time. The bill also called for a new setback line to be drawn, using some pseudoscientific rationale.

They picked a time forty years ago and decided, for some arcane reason, that where the shoreline was then, was to be the limit of development allowed on the South Carolina coast in the future. Why not use 50 years or 200 years or five years ago as a guideline? I have never been able to find out their rationale for selecting that arbitrary time span. This line was to be reviewed every five years and could be redrawn if the Coastal Council so decreed.

Even now, it was not certain that my lots would be affected by the legislation. I would have to wait and see where the line fell. The bad news wasn't long in coming. They got me. Not only did the line encompass my lots, but it took in the street behind my lots. Not only was my property included in this new asinine law, but they had taken away any possible economic use. It was by zoning, restricted to construction of a single family residence only. There were no alternate uses that would justify spending the kind of money for the lots that I had already spent. The state of South Carolina, with this new law, had just destroyed millions of dollars worth of value for which her citizens had been working hundreds of years to create. What was going on here?

After the initial shock wore off, the question was what to do now? I had several choices, none of them good. I could rush out and try to get a couple of construction permits. This was a bad business decision forced by government interference with the market. I could ask that the line be redrawn which meant that I had to take advantage of the administrative remedy that the state offered. Of course, there was no guarantee that after spending a lot of money I would be granted any relief. Or, I could do what was right and fight this unconstitutional law in court.

The first alternative could become a trap. It would not be based on market considerations, but on a reaction to an illegal law. The second alternative could also become a quagmire. The company drawing the line was the same company that had only two years ago been hired to do an erosion study for Wild Dunes. However, even knowing these people personally was no guarantee that, in the end, I would be successful in having the line redrawn favorably. My options were narrowing rapidly.

The third route was the most dangerous and posed the greatest potential financial hardship. It also gave me the opportunity to do what was right and perhaps strike a small blow for regaining some lost freedom for my country. If they got away with this legalized theft, where would it end? What and who would be next? I felt that I owed it to the people of the country and of my state. They had made my good fortune possible by allowing me the freedom to live the American Dream. Now that avenue of freedom was being choked off for others who would not have the same opportunities. The right to acquire and use property had to be defended. The state had drawn a line in the sand in more ways than one. I could fold and walk away or stand up for myself and every other property owner in this country. I know this may sound corny to some, but my father and mother, Big John Wayne, Charles Starrett, Randolf Scott, Gene Autry, and all my other boyhood heros had taught me to fight for the principles in which I believed. Put that way, my decision was made. I called Attorney Gedney Howe.

Now Gedney is quite a character. His father,

"Big Gedney" was the leader of the Democrat Party in Charleston for many years. During the 1940s, 1950s and 1960s he was one of the most powerful political figures in the state. I had known "Little Gedney" in college. We attended The University of South Carolina at the same time. He had returned to Charleston after completing law school, also at USC, and had carved out a flamboyant, and lucrative career for himself. In dealings with the state, Gedney had a very good reputation for representing the winning side.

Gedney has a colorful lifestyle. He had just finished remodeling the old John C. Calhoun Mansion on Meeting Street in downtown Charleston. It is a beautiful place. He also drives a Rolls Royce, one of the few existing in the state. It's not a bad set of wheels. His office is in the oldest, most historic section of Charleston. It is loaded with beautiful art work and the furnishings are lavish. I sat down in those surroundings with Gedney to discuss the lots, the law, and constitutional philosophy.

He agreed that what the state had done was unconstitutional. He cautioned, however, that the tide of environmentalism was running very strongly in South Carolina and that similar situations had occurred under other laws and the landowners had lost. This was not going to be a walk on the beach. I thought that perhaps he was now leading me into a discussion of the fee arrangement. After all, this was supposed to be one of the most conservative states in the union. But no longer, I soon found out to my dismay. It seemed that my South Carolina state government had been taken over by a bunch of power hungry bureaucrats.

Gedney had called in another attorney who was considered an expert in the field of environmental regulations, Ellison Smith. I had known Ellison since my deep sea fishing days back in Garden City and Murrell's Inlet. As a matter of fact, he went along on our maiden fishing trip aboard the Rebel Yell. He was also good friends with my old buddy, Johnny Ball. South Carolina is a small state.

I liked and respected Ellison. Since he didn't practice real estate law, and up until then, I had only needed real estate lawyers, our paths had not crossed since I had moved to Charleston. Ellison's family originally came from Lee County as does my family. The area is the heart of cotton growing in South Carolina. As a matter of fact, Ellison's grandfather was named "Cotton Ed Smith." He was a very successful cotton farmer from Lynchburg.

Lynchburg is located in the lower part of Lee County while Turkey Creek is located in the upper portion of the county. "Cotton Ed " was the only United States Senator to ever be elected from Lee County. After his long and illustrious career in Washington, the family left Lee County.

The old Smith Family plantation, Tanglewood,

was just bought by an artist cousin of mine from Lynchburg, Jerry Locklair. Tanglewood is a beautiful place located just off I-95 which runs through the southern portion of the county. Jerry wants to use it as an historical draw for Florida-bound tourists. The more people that stop to visit Tanglewood, the more paintings Jerry can sell. If Jerry succeeds in his venture, then private enterprise will save an historical site without government intervention.

Gedney and Ellison agreed that it was as good a case as possible with which to challenge the Beach Front Management Act. We discussed for the first time, but for me certainly not the last, the different theories of law that could possibly be used for our attack. Was the act unconstitutional or, if not, how could we make them pay me for the value that had been taken by the enforcement of the act?

I had briefly harbored aspirations of becoming a lawyer myself, and had even passed the entrance exam at the University of South Carolina Law School. My sister, April was an attorney with the very prestigious McNair Firm in Columbia. I had also dealt with lawyers now for many years on real estate closings. With all of these connections, I, at least, understand their terminology. However, I had never studied, or really discussed, legal theories behind the law.

I had read the constitution, and had taken civics classes in high school and college. I was an international relations major at the University of South Carolina where we studied different forms of governments around the world. But, I certainly was not prepared for the rude education that was coming. I thought that I was relatively intelligent and well educated, but soon realized how naive I was about the American Judicial System. I had read the Bill of Rights and thought that the language was plain and simple, and meant what it said. But I didn't realize a priestly class was needed to interpret and intercede on my behalf with the "law gods" who have taken over our legal system.

The conversation then turned to the fee arrangement. Gedney always works on a contingency basis. There is, of course, more risk for a lawyer that way, but if successful, it is much more lucrative than a simple fee arrangement. With that in mind, I remembered Gedney's Calhoun Mansion, his plush offices, and that Rolls Royce. Obviously, this was a measure of his success. That was the clincher for me. I felt that the no win, no pay doctrine was a good way to keep their heads and hearts in the right place. We settled on a middle of the road percentage plus expenses.

The two of them agreed to split the contingency

fee and to share cost on a 50\50 basis. We agreed to meet again and concluded the first meeting on a cautiously optimistic note. Within a couple of days a letter from Gedney arrived, and enclosed was an agreement for the fee arrangement. I read it carefully and decided to sign it so that we could move on with the process. With the signing of this agreement, the die was cast. We began to prepare the case now known as *Lucas versus the South Carolina Coastal Council.*

4

Judge Paterson's A Good Man

OR:

How I Fought The Law and I Won

The Fifth Amendment of the United States Constitution reads as follows: *No person shall be held to answer for a capital or otherwise infamous crime, unless on a presentment or indictment of a grand jury, except in cases arising in the land or naval forces, or in the militia, when in actual service in time of war or public danger; nor shall any person be subject for the same offense to be twice put in jeopardy of life or limb; nor shall be compelled in any criminal case to be a witness against himself, nor be deprived of life, liberty, or property, without due process of law; nor shall private property be taken for public use, without just compensation.*

Now that's not hard to understand. If you break out the part about property rights, the language becomes even plainer because it's shorter and requires less of an attention span.

The part dealing with property rights says that *"no person shall be deprived of life, liberty, or property, without due process of law; nor shall private property be taken for public use, without just compensation."*

Gedney and Ellison wasted no time in preparing the lawsuit. Ellison was responsible for producing the legal theory that became the basis for our suit. He decided not to attack the law under the due process part of the Fifth Amendment even though the way the Beachfront Management Act was written, and the stated reasons for its enactment were clearly a violation of the "due process clause" of the Fifth Amendment. There was no threat to public safety and therefore not a pressing public need. Although the Act mentioned public safety, the main rationale was to supposedly "protect" the beaches, in order to promote the tourism industry in the state. This was mainly benefit bestowing and not protection providing as required by due process. The lawyer for the state even argues this point in our first trial. The due process clause has been out of favor for many years in the courts of this country and that is a shame. The courts seem to feel that if the state legislatures pass a law, that is enough to constitute "due process" under the Fifth Amendment.

It seems that the reason the courts frown on acting on the due process clause is that they don't want to be in opposition to the democratically elected legislature. They feel that getting legislation enacted into law and signed by the Governor is due process enough.

I have another opinion on that subject after feeling the effects of the lack of due process protection afforded at present by our government. After all, this was not just any piece of legislation that we were getting ready to attack. This was the gem of the South Carolina legislature's environmental legacy and was very popular with the voters statewide.

It was particularly popular with people who didn't own property in immediate danger of being taken by the government. So, it seemed futile to attack the law on the due process clause.

I was appalled by this revelation. I had read my rights under the Fifth Amendment before and thought that the language was pretty clear. Then Ellison explained to me that the courts were ignoring the constitution, particularly in cases that were popular with the public. I had not expected this kind of political activism in the courts of my state.

This had happened before in America on other emotional issues. Just because a majority of the people think something is right doesn't make it right. That's why this country is not a pure democracy, but a republic with constitutional guarantees for minorities. The Constitution is in place to protect minorities from injustice. That was what the civil rights movement was supposedly all about; protection of a minority from oppression by the majority. Now, I was feeling first hand the lack of constitutional protection and the oppression by the majority opinion in the state of South Carolina.

With the due process part of the Fifth Amendment out of action, that left the just compensation clause. If they were going to take the property it seemed that we could not stop them from doing so. There was a better chance that we could make them pay for the taking. The act itself was silent on compensation. The state legislature had just assumed that no payment would be due. Ellison then patiently explained that even that part of the Fifth Amendment was not a sure fire winner. It seems that in some cases, the courts had also been reluctant to go against the legislative body even in the just compensation area. If you had remaining value in your property after a governmental body had finished with you, then chances were, you wouldn't get "just compensation."

The advantage that we had with this particular case was that there was no ambiguity in residual value here. My lots had no remaining value. There was only one use allowed under the zoning in Wild Dunes and that was to build single family residences on those lots. That one activity had been clearly prohibited by the new law. Since the line effectively prohibited building on any part of my lots, I had no economic use whatsoever of even a part of my land.

They were the only two lots, out of the two hundred lots, affected by this act in the entire state of South Carolina that were taken entirely by this harsh new law. The other lots had been reduced in buildable area, but were still usable and therefore had a residual value (even though I believe that they should be compensated for any lost value). I had become the sacrificial lamb and was on the butcher's block. Thus, we were in a position to spotlight our legal theory in a clear, concise, and stark light. We would ask for monetary compensation from the state for a taking. Although the state did not take actual title to the lots, they had taken all of the real value from the land and from my bank account. For this type of taking, the language of the Just Compensation clause is unambiguous. This law took the value of my property for a public use, therefore, it owed me just compensation. After all of our deliberations it had boiled down to this: we would not attack the body of the law itself as unconstitutional, but would try to get compensation for the enforcement of the act as called for in the Fifth Admendment.

The lawsuit was prepared and filed in early 1989. A court date was set for August of that year. We lined up all of our witnesses and all of the necessary backup documents, and had a formidable case to present to the court. The facts of the case were pretty simple as was the legal theory behind our case. It was clear the law took my property and the Constitution said that I was owed just compensation for that taking. After we filed our lawsuit, the state answered and, of course, denied any liability.

Soon the news media got wind of the case and the statewide publicity battle began. Editorials soon came out in each of the newspapers of the state. Most of the editorials backed the state's position. A few seemed troubled by the potential abuse of power by the state, but in general, they all felt that the state had the right to tell anyone not to use their property simply because it was near the beach, regardless of the damage to the individual or to the constitution. After the editorials, all manner of experts were given space in the newspapers to tell the people that there was a pressing need for this state law. If I were to prevail, all manner of calamities would befall the various governmental bodies of the country.

The coastal council spokesmen were regularly quoted by the press. The environmentalists were given space to write about the "eroding" coastline. These "scare" articles, along with graphic pictures depicting shoreline problems, were in the news almost every week. The environmental spin doctors were out in full force. There were several sightings by environmental experts of the end of the natural world hovering just off the coast of Charleston. They commented on the case ad nauseam. Not only did they appear in the newspapers, but on radio talk shows and television stations as well. Gedney and Ellison wanted me to keep my mouth shut. It was good advice not to argue with people who buy ink by the barrel or have unlimited radio and television exposure.

Gedney advised me not to say anything publicly that might prejudice any potential judge against our case. So, I bit my lip and only spouted the legal line that my lawyers allowed. And a very muted line it was. Each side then filed legal briefs and listed potential witnesses. Depositions were taken and documents were submitted and studied thoroughly. The state listed only a couple of expert witnesses. Our list of witnesses was short too, but very well qualified to testify in their respective fields.

The court date arrived and our side showed up early for the legal fireworks. We were ready for battle. There wasn't a big crowd of spectators in the court room, just a few members of the media and several interested environmentalists. There were several interested and concerned property owners who were there to offer me their moral support. Martha and I went into the court-room and greeted our witnesses. We had lined up some good ones.

David Stevens was an engineer who was very familiar with barrier islands. David had been in-volved on the Isle of Palms, working on beach renourishment projects and on the construction of the Isle of Palms Marina. He was very familiar with the recent hydrological history of the island. Our other expert witness was from Atlanta. He was the appraiser who had helped with my pur-chase of Wild Dunes in 1984, Don Pardue. Don had done most of the appraisal work on the is-land during the past few years and certainly knew more about the values there than anyone else around. Because of the work that Don had done in Wild Dunes, he been asked to appraise prop-erty on other sea islands from North Carolina to Florida. Don had become the foremost expert on values for beachfront resort properties in the southeast. He had worked on properties in pri-vate resorts with amenity packages like Wild

Dunes, as well as regular beachfront properties. And, of course, I was to get my turn in the witness box. I knew quite a bit about that island myself.

The morning was clear and warm. The courtroom was small and the hum of the air conditioner was audible. We were milling around the courtroom when a small guy with gold rimmed glasses approached me. I could tell by the way he was dressed and by the type of large briefcase that he was lugging, that he was an attorney. He was blonde and smiled pleasantly as he offered me his hand. I must admit that my first impulse was to help that little guy with that huge load he was carrying. He introduced himself as Cotton Harness, attorney for the South Carolina Coastal Council.

He told me that he was sorry that we had met under these conditions, but that he looked forward to meeting me at another time under more pleasant circumstances. With him, politely, but definitely identified as the enemy, I decided not to offer to help him with his briefcase. I hoped to be involved in helping him get rid of an even more difficult burden: trying to defend an unconstitutional law that even he didn't really believe was fair.

In spite of who he was, I found that I couldn't help but like Cotton. However, I was not happy with his "boss," the state, and remained on my guard, despite his congenial bearing. I said hello in a very sober manner. Cotton continued to talk and I got the distinct impression that he was uncomfortable with his part in this attempted robbery by the state. It was as if he had been told that it was alright to rob me, because it was for the benefit of the rest of the people of the state. After all, building a house on those lots would be a clear threat to the public or so he had been told and later forced to argue in court. He argued the state's case with a straight face as we shall soon see.

I got the feeling that Cotton wasn't convinced that I was really public enemy number one, but just some poor guy that had been caught up in the machinery of government. So he was being nice to the sacrificial lamb. But the lamb was not going to be sacrificed willingly or without a good fight. I saw Cotton as the upfront man in this theft of my property.

I was trying to think of the proper way to approach this guy. I didn't want to be too friendly, even though I thought he was probably a nice fellow.

On the other hand, if I had a reluctant adversary, then perhaps it wouldn't be smart to harden his position by being rude to him. I also didn't want him to think that it was alright to persecute and steal from innocent people, even if it was in the name of the Great State of South Carolina. What to do?

I decided to be distant, but pleasant. This would hopefully allow him to try and show me that he wasn't really so bad, but was just doing his job. That's what they had said at Nurenberg just after World War II, as well.

About that time I was saved from saying more by the bailiff's cry of "all rise." Then the door behind the big raised desk opened and in walked Judge Paterson. He moved quickly to take his seat high up on the bench.

The tension level in the courtroom had now risen perceptively. All eyes were fixed on the man in black. This was not going to be a jury trial. This man was going to be the jury as well as the judge. That made him doubly powerful in this case.

As it turned out, his ruling was to have an impact on the entire nation. However, that was to come years later. But now, Court was in session.

The trial was not a long drawn out affair. It lasted only a day. We began the proceedings with a short statement by Ellison Smith. What follows is taken from the actual court record of the case. I think that it will be enough to give you the essence of the day.

Looking back on this testimony, I have even found some humorous statements that were made by both sides. So I offer to my readers selected portions of the actual testimony and comments from the August 1989 trial of Lucas v. South Carolina Coastal Council.

TEXT FROM TRIAL I

Page 8

> Ellison Smith: "May it please the Court, Your Honor, I'm Ellison Smith. We have alleged that the South Carolina Coastal Council has taken Mr. Lucas' property in violation of Article One, Section 13, of the South Carolina Constitution, and Amendment Five of the United States Constitution.
>
> So what we have done is we have brought a direct constitutional action for inverse condemnation which the law of South Carolina allows us to do. If we are correct that the South Carolina Coastal Council has taken Mr. Lucas's private property for public purposes, then the Constitution of the state of South Carolina and the Constitution of the United States of America require that just compensation be paid.
>
> Now, Mr. Harness has suggested to the Court and his answer seeks to require us to go back to the very administrative agency that we believe created the problem in the first instance. We're not interested in doing that.

"We believe that in the contest of the case now in front of this Court, if in fact the activity of the South Carolina Coastal Council has amounted to a taking of private property for public purposes, there is one remedy and one remedy only, and that is the payment of just compensation."

Nicely done Mr. Smith!
Now It was Cotton's turn at bat.

Page 10

Cotton Harness: "If I could be allowed to proceed, although they apparently do not feel compelled to make an opening argument, I think from the State's point of view, it's important that we set forth our position, because it is admitted in the stipulations that, in fact, the gentleman cannot build a habitable structure under the current law that the South Carolina Coastal Council is administering at this time."☞

Page 13

Harness: "The Act was passed for the protection, preservation, restoration, enhancement of the beaches in the system, by retreat, by comprehensive planning, and by use of nourishment where appropriate."☞

Page 14

Harness: "As we will point out, he can use it for some things. The Coastal Council wouldn't prevent

☞ If you are swayed by this argument, turn to page 252 and read about the hypocritical actions taken by the state when *their* money was at risk. —D.L.

him from—I'm not trying to be facetious, but we wouldn't prevent him from putting a trailer or a tent on it or having some use of the property because the fact of the matter is we regulate construction of habitable structures.

Now, given the fact that we have a high public purpose here, and that is to protect the beach dune system, protect the people from loss of life and limb, in looking to future generations to be sure that we have a beach present for people, and that what we have is not overbuilt and destroyed by the desire of man and the force of the ocean☞, we don't believe there is a taking in this case. We don't believe it for the following reasons:

In unconstitutional taking cases, the Court can award just compensation subject to the discussion we just had recently about amending my answer, but the Court has to use a balancing process, and that process is to look at the importance of the public purpose in preventing a harm.

In this case, the harm being a number of things. Where people build close to the Atlantic Ocean, the public has to bail them out in terms of flood insurance; in terms of emergency money and loans from the government for them to reconstruct; in the placing of nourishment and temporarily damaging the environment; in disturbing the habitat of animals; in disturbing the beach people might be able to use because in eroding beaches the beaches tend to move back; and also in the sense of the loss of life and property. Not only this gentleman's life and property but also people behind him because in hurricanes buildings often blow into property landward of the beachfront property.☞

So there is a high public purpose there. In addition to that, we believe that there is a requirement of the State of South Carolina, that in order to determine if the property has been taken, you not only look at the public purpose and how high the public purpose is, but you also look to see whether the land is suitable for the use intended.

We will demonstrate to the Court today, that the property is not suitable for construction☞; that it is in an area that is extremely volatile, despite the fact that there are houses on either side of the property; that the location of this property is in so perilous a position, that it really is not usable☞ and in fact we will take issue concerning the appraisals that while they appraise the property at well over Five Hundred Thousand Dollars, that the gentleman, we'll stipulate paid almost half a million Dollars for these lots, that what he bought was a pig in a poke.

Now, that has to be balanced together with — I agree with the degree of economic loss, and if the Court determines that the economic loss the gentleman has experienced—if you determine he has experienced a loss, you balance it against the measure or level of the public interest here; that what the Court should do is, as I mentioned earlier, allow the Council to do one of two things: *Either pay the man for his property or allow him to build something on his property.* *

Either allow him to construct something there or pay compensation. The State should be given that opportunity to withdraw the harsh application of any Act, and then the issue really comes down to whether or not we owe this gentleman for temporary–a temporary taking or temporary damages.

Your Honor, in trying to save time for the Court, given the complexity of this case, the attorneys on both sides have sat down in lengthy meetings and tried to come up with some fact stipulations to make the Court's job easier."

What follows is some, but not all of those stipulations.

Page 19

Harness: "The current law prevents construction of any habitable structures or recreational amenities. That includes swimming pools, tennis courts and such, on the subject lot.

The next one would be that the beach is primarily affected by Dewees Inlet — that's the inlet which is adjacent to this island, and is generally accreted at

---

* I couldn't believe this was the State's argument.

a rate of two point four feet per year—that the beach is actually accreting at that rate.

However, that erosion does occur at the beach in question.

The next one is that the subject lots have houses on either side.

The next one, would be that the intended use for Lot 22 and 24, construction of single family homes: and the Coastal Council agrees that any application for permit to build would have been denied."

We then called our first witness.

Page 25

(Ellison Smith questioning David Stevens)

Q. All right, sir. Now, you've got some other lines on this, plat, Mr. Stevens. Would you explain to the Court what those are?

A. Well, we went to — Mr. Smith, I went to the Coastal Council to verify these lines and I in turn put them on this to use for Exhibit 1. This is the mean high water line for the project, and the distance back to the lot is approximately — it ranges from three hundred ten feet to three hundred fifty feet. This is basically in this area.

Q. So how far is it from the corner of Lot 24 to the mean high water mark?

A. Three hundred forty feet.

Q. And how far is it from – let's call this the western corner of Lot 22 – to the mean high water mark?

A. Three hundred ten feet. This line was given to us by the Coastal Council. The mean high water line. We were trying to establish and did establish that the lots' seaward corner was over the length of a football field away from the high water mark.

Page 38

(Gedney Howe questioning David Lucas)

Q. So you had an opportunity to invest anywhere?

A. That's correct.

Q. And you had the pick of all the lots on the beach?

A. The ones that were left, yes.

Q. A pick of undeveloped lots?

A. That's correct.

Q. And you had all the background and knowledge that had accumulated over the years?

A. Correct.

Q. And you chose these two?

A. That's correct.

Q. Why?

A. Well, we had always taken into consideration the movement of the ocean, the Atlantic Ocean. I mean, it's obvious that there is always a risk of a big storm or a hurricane. One of the things that really attracted us to the island and investment on the island was the studies we had done. When we put lots up for sale or when we developed condominiums we always took in the latest data that we had. We didn't just go out and say we're going to stick these lots one foot from the critical line. We never did that sort of thing.

The Finches were very responsible developers and they were cognizant of the fact that there could be some liability if they were not responsible.

There were studies done. There were ongoing studies done. Markers were placed out on the beach so they kept tabs on erosion and accretion, and every study that I'm aware of, said that the beach was an accretion area - - a growing beach; that over the past fifteen hundred years the land has built oceanward, but that there would be sometimes intermittent and temporary erosion during that period of time.

I don't think you could equate the — every beach as being an eroding beach in the State of South

Carolina. I would contend there are certain very bad places where erosion takes place, but I don't see how you can treat every place the same.

(End of my testimony.)

Here, I was trying to show that contrary to what the state was saying, the lots were not bought as a pig in a poke but after careful analysis of the available information.

Page 78

(Harness questioning Don Pardue our appraiser, on cross examination about present market value.)

Q. And isn't it true that sometimes you buy property and speculate on the property, maybe in this case hoping the Beach Front Management Act would be overturned or the Legislature would come to its senses and do something a little less harsh?

A. Well, I guess ...

Mr. Howe: That's our line — can we adopt that, Your Honor?

The Court: Is there any — your questions are that they can buy this providing nothing can be built on it. Well, nothing can be built on it.

Mr.Harness: I understand that, Your Honor. What we're trying to do, Your Honor, is at least see if there are some uses the property can be put to.

The Court: There would be no motivation right now for anybody to buy it to keep construction from going up.

Mr.Harness: Only to purchase it for the purpose of having their view unencumbered.

The Court: The view will be unencumbered. They can't build anything. Right?

Mr. Harness: I understand.

The Court: Okay. Unencumbered — I don't see why anybody would buy it so it would be unencumbered if it can't be encumbered.

Mr.Harness: I guess, Your Honor, my questions fall on deaf ears. I will just sort of stop at this point in time.

The Court: It's not falling on deaf ears. I just am interested in — if you've got a point, I'd like to — I mean, I'm missing it.

Mr.Harness: We intend to put in through our expert, is put in testimony that there is a salvage value. I'm trying to discover if this gentleman believes there is a salvage value which he has said he does not in essence — he has not dealt with property similarly situated in the past to give an answer. I was just trying to thrash that out and see.

A. If I may comment. As I stated earlier, I feel like the property has no value at all. I think maybe the thought here might be, Your Honor, that with the impact of this beach line, nothing can be done to this property.

Now, a knowledgeable adjoining property owner, knowing that nothing can ever be developed here, would not pay any money for this because he's going to get it for free, so to speak.

Why would he spend any money at all if no development can be placed on this? As a matter of fact, in a way the individual that owns that middle (home) has far and large some very extreme fortune in my opinion.

The Court: I understand that the stipulation was that the boardwalks or some other temporary structure can be put out there but is there a restriction — I'm sure that...

Mr. Harness: Your Honor, I don't have any evidence of that, standing before you today.

The Court: ... that no temporary structures can be used out there.

Mr. Harness: I can't speak to that. I don't know what Isle of Palms — what their restrictive covenants would do. I only know what the Coastal Council would do.

The Court: All right.

Mr. Harness: I have no further questions, Your Honor.

Page 81

Mr. Harness: Your Honor, we would move for directed verdict at this time based upon the following grounds: The Plaintiff must prove that he is entitled to damages. Really it is a two-pronged test.

They don't challenge— they have not challenged that the purpose of the Act is valid.

They don't present any evidence showing that there might be some use of the property; that is, put some temporary structure on there, albeit it may be a lot less satisfactory than building a house.

Our opinion and our position is they would have to show there was absolutely and totally no use.

It is our position that they haven't shown that the Isle of Palms would preclude a trailer or tent on it and they do have some use of the property still left, although from our point of view it would be a walkway and a deck that we would permit.

That, taken together with the use of a trailer, implemented – and they again have presented no evidence to point otherwise, would afford them some opportunity for use of the property and not a total deprivation of use of the property.

In addition to that, we do not believe that they have demonstrated that the property is suitable for the purpose intended.☞ There are houses built along that stretch of the beach.

Now, granted, they have constructed houses in the area. They have been constructed over a period of time prior to passing of the Beachfront Management Act, but in fact this is the very reason the Beachfront Management Act was passed, to essentially require people to use a little more foresight in constructing or developing–doing developments and constructing structures.☞

Based on that, we feel that we are entitled to a directed verdict.

Mr. Smith: Very briefly, Your Honor. Mr. Lucas, as I recall, testified that in his–that the property cannot be used for anything.

What we are now dealing with is a man who in 1986 bought two lots, one for Four Hundred Seventy-Five Thousand Dollars and one for Five Hundred Thousand Dollars in December of 1986. There is ample testimony.

At the time he purchased those lots both lots

were suitable, according to all of the testimony, for single family residential development. They are suitable now for single family residential development, but for the imposition by the State of South Carolina of the two lines the Court has seen.

There is no impediment about building on these two lots. Nobody has suggested to the contrary, but for these two lines. Probably the best evidence of that is the substantial house next door, houses on either side, and there is almost a hundred yards from the edge of the lot line to the Atlantic waters, the high water mark of the Atlantic Ocean.

Now, Mr. Harness is suggesting to the Court that the property has to have no value for a regulatory taking to take place.

All of our testimony today has been that it has no value. The law of the State of South Carolina is a little different, Your Honor. Years ago, the Supreme Court of South Carolina said:

> Property in a thing consists not merely in its ownership and possession but in the unrestricted right of use, enjoyment and disposal. Anything which destroys one or more of these elements of property, to that extent destroys the property itself.

It must be conceded that the substantial value of a property lies in its use. If the right of use be denied, the value of the property is annihilated and the ownership is rendered a barren right.

The constitutional prohibition against taking private property for public use without just compensation must have been intended to protect all of the essential elements of ownership which make property valuable, including, of course, the right of user and the right of enjoyment."

That's still the law in the State of South Carolina, Your Honor, and I think the motion for directed verdict should be denied.

The Court: I'm going to deny your motion, Mr. Harness.

Mr. Harness: Your Honor, we have three witnesses that we'll put up today.

The Court: Had you all planned on trying this for most of the day?

Mr. Harness: We would like to get it over with if we can. I think from the State's point of view we have so many of these cases that are lurking out there that we'd like to get one done and decided so the Council has some direction."

We adjourned for lunch at this point and resumed with the state trying to prove its case—whatever that was.

Page 85

(Harness questioning Christopher Jones, a witness for the state)

Q. What do you do for a living?

A. I'm a coastal engineer.

Q. How long have you been a coastal engineer?

A. A total of about twelve years, three years in South Carolina.

Q. And for whom do you work right now?

A. Coastal Science and Engineering, Inc.

Q. Now, for the Judge, would you explain to him what it means to be an expert in coastal processes?

A. An expert in coastal processes is someone who understands those natural or man-made forces that affect the shoreline, including the effects of waves, tides, currents, storms on structures.

Q. All right, sir. What structures do you mean?

A. We can be talking about seawalls and abutments or erosion control types of devices. We can also talk about jetties and other structures at tidal inlets.

Q. Man-made buildings?

A. Yes.

Q. Now, what does it mean to be an expert in shorefront management?

A. I think an expert in shorefront management is someone who first understands the natural processes that affect the shoreline and, secondly, is concerned with the appropriate use of that shoreline so that the upland development is not threatened by erosion or storms, such that we will protect the recreational beach.

Q. Okay. Does that include determination on the suitability of land for construction purposes?

A. In many cases, yes.

Q. All right, sir, and have you had experience in both of those areas in terms of your education?

A. Yes, sir.

Page 116

(Continued questioning of Jones by Harness)

Q. Is it your opinion that houses and structures along the east end of the Isle of Palms have been threatened in the past by erosion? ✑

A. I think they have.

Q. Is it your opinion that it will continue to be

threatened?

A. Yes.

Q. Answer any questions that Mr. Howe might have for you.

A. I have one more slide.

Q. Let's look at it then.

A. This is a March first of 1983 slide showing the house at Lot 20 which is two houses to the west of the Lucas property. You can see this was taken, I think, during an emergency shoal scraping done under permit of the Coastal Council, and without the scraping and subsequent nourishment this house would have been certainly threatened by erosion.

Page 117

(Howe questioning Jones)

Q. Mr. Harness kept asking you to tell us what was going to happen with absolute certainty. You can't tell us anything with absolute certainty?

A. No.

Q. That's not usually words that are used in the Courtroom because we just don't ever know what's going to happen with absolute certainty, do we?

A. No.

Q. You do know that this sandbar is—this is where it's located now?

A. Yes.

Q. And that it is moving out in this area in front of the Lucas property?

A. Yes.

Q. And Mr. Lucas's property is in fact accreting at a very significant rate right now?

A. At the present time I think the Lucas property is, let's say stable or accreting at something near the long term rate.

Q. Now, again, this sand bar we're talking about— with a reasonable degree of certainty, this sand bar is going to be sort of easing off along the front of this property and will represent an accretion to his property?

A. I think most of the accretion will actually occur further down at the east end of Dunecrest Lane in the vicinity of Lots 8 and 9.

Q. But the way for it to get there is to go past the Lucas property?

A. No. The Lucas property is further to the west.

Q. Where is the Lucas property?

A. The Lucas property is right in here, on either side of this particular house. The erosion that is associated with this shoal attachment was principally further east along Beachwood East and Dunecrest Lane.

Q. Did you tell us on direct that you anticipated this shoal 'evening' out in this area?

A. What will happen is this shoal will move on-shore and will tend to even out the area in here which is eroding.

Q. Now, you said a couple of things that I liked so I'm going to repeat them. You said this part of the island is in fact accreting?

A. Yes, sir.

Q. And you talked about it having a long term accretional effect?

A Yes.

Q. And that means that the beach, the island itself, will get larger and larger as if to project out into the ocean?

A. Over the long term.

Q. It is the opposite of erosion?

A. True.

Q. And you agree that this island generally, and

this portion of the island over the long term, is in fact an accretional island?

A. Over the long term.

Q. Now, who is Tim Canner?

A. Tim Canner is President of the firm for which I work.

Q. He's your boss?

A. Yes.

Q. And how long has he been your boss?

A. Three years.

Q. What is the name of the firm?

A. Coastal Science and Engineering.

Q. And he's the President. Is he also a stockholder?

A. Yes.

Q. And are you a stockholder?

A. No.

Q. And within the chain of command, you are under him?

A. Yes.

Q. He's above you, but between you and him—do you report directly to him?

A. Yes.

Q. What is your title?

A. Coastal engineer.

Q. And what is his title?

A. Coastal geologist.

Q. And President of..

A. Of the firm.

Q. Now has he had experience with this island?

A. Yes, he has.

Q. And does his experience predate yours?

A. Yes.

Q. And would you think his experience is extensive?

A. Yes

Q. And would you think his ability is substantial?

A Yes.

Q. And I'm not going to ask you to disagree with the boss too much on the record. It's not good for long term accretion of your job. Are you familiar with this document?

A. Yes sir, I am.

Q. What is this document?

A. I'm not sure of its origin, but it's a pamphlet

put together I think about 1984, describing the shoreline processes at Wild Dunes for potential property owners.

Q. And it was written after this erosion, this short term erosion problem, wasn't it?

A. During or after the shoal attachment?

Q. If you look at the back page, it says for further information please call Tim Canner, is that correct?

A. Yes.

Q. Did he in fact participate in preparation of that document?

A. I suppose he did.

Q. It is your understanding he was in fact the primary author of this document?

A. I really don't know.

Q. That's not your understanding that it is prepared by his company?

A. No, I know that he assisted, but I can't attest to his exact involvement in writing the final copy.

Q. He worked for the Research Planning Institute at that time?

A. That's true.

Q. And the only name that appears in connection with Research Planning Institute is whose?

A. Is his.

Q. Nobody else listed?

A. True.

Q. Now do you agree with his statement that during 1982 and 1983...

Mr. Harness: Your Honor, I'm going to object. I want to at least look at it before he starts..

Mr. Howe: Sure, It's all yellowed out for you.

Q. Do you agree with his statement that during 1982 and 1983, an incident of localized erosion occurred in the general area of Mariner's Walk and Sea Grove Villas at Wild Dunes, and the incident temporarily affected less than ten percent of the beach.

A. True

Q. Okay, and do you agree that, quote-quote, interestingly, during the same year in which this incident of erosion occurred, there was a net accretion on Wild Dunes; in fact, the beach has grown quite steadily for fifteen hundred years?

A. True.

Q. And we look over on the third page on the over-

LUCAS VS. THE GREEN MACHINE

all accretion, and do you agree with the statement, that historical information dating back to 1886, aerial photographs and scientific studies help us understand the changes in the shoreline of the Isle of Palms; scientists believe the northeast end of the Isle of Palms, where Wild Dunes and Beach and Racquet Club is located, has accreted for the past fifteen hundred years; the theory is supported by visible ridges viewed from the air.

In other words, as you fly over the Isle of Palms, changes in vegetation clearly outline previous shorelines.

A. True

Q. There is a section in here on localized erosion. That's what you were telling us sometimes happens in conjunction with the accretion?

A. Yes.

Q. Do you agree that the accretional effects of shore migration at Wild Dunes gives us a very positive picture of overall changes in the shoreline? However, occasionally in a cycle of nature we can experience localized areas of temporary erosion which can occur even within a portion of the beach which is experiencing general accretion?

A. True.

Q. The northeast end of the Isle of Palms has built seaward during the past fifteen hundred years because of continuous supply of sand from Dewees Inlet from the north?

A. True.

Q. The long-range effect then is accretion for the entire stretch of the beach. Occasionally, though, the temporary erosion is severe enough to require immediate action?

A. True.

Q. On the future projects, although localized erosion can occur, again in the natural process of inlet and offshore shoals, erosion at Wild Dunes has been a temporary process and a minor occurrence when viewed beside the overall accretional trends of the island; Isle Of Palms has built seaward for the past few thousand years due to a surplus of sediment transported by way of tidal limits; studies by RPI indicate the shoreline will continue to fluctuate into the future but that overall Wild Dunes will have a healthy and beautiful beach.

A. True.

Q. Do you know, other than the Beachfront Management Act, of any other legal impediments that would keep Mr. Lucas from building single family residences on Lot 22 and Lot 24?

A. I don't know of any.

Q. And are there, in fact, houses on both sides, and a house in the middle of those lots?

A. I don't know of any other impediments.

Q. That's all.

(Redirect examination by Mr. Harness)

Q. Does this document change your opinion that these houses will be threatened by the ocean from time to time?☜

A. It does not change my opinion. The document states in several places that the island has been accretional and that is over the long term a correct statement. The document also states, however, that it is subject to erosion, albeit temporary. Whether temporary or not, I think it would have the same impact on structures that were in the way.

Q. What is temporary?

A. Usually—I should say with the shoal attachment we've observed in the 1980s we may be talking about something that occurs over a period of years. Maybe two years to three years.

Q. So there is a possibility that exists that the shore

line would return to the 1963 point and stay there for several years?

A. That possibility does exist.

Mr. Howe: I would object to that and ask that it be stricken. Possibilities just aren't admissible in the law.

The Court: I sustain the objection.

Mr. Harness: Nothing further, Your Honor.

Page 139

(Harness questioning Mr. Christopher Donato)

Q. Have you had experience in appraising real estate on Isle of Palms?

A. Yes, Sir.

Q. And would you tell me roughly how many appraisals you have done?

A. Gee, that's tough to come up with, Mr. Harness. Probably in the neighborhood of fifty appraisals over the years, varying from either a single family residence to a development project.

Q. Have you appraised properties similarly situated; that is, beachfront property?

A. Yes Sir.

Q. And where have you done this? Just on the Isle Of Palms or elsewhere?

A. Elsewhere.

Q. Now, we retained you to do some work for us, and what was your charge by Coastal Council?

A. Well, Coastal Council asked me to estimate the market value of the two Lucas lots on June 30, 1988, which is my understanding of the implementation of the 1988 Beachfront Management Act.

The appraisal was to be exclusive of any restrictions imposed by that Beachfront Act, as well as exclusive of any consideration that the lots may be unsuitable for construction.

Q. So you didn't deal with whether or not erosion was a factor in evaluating the property?

A. No, sir, I didn't

Q. What was the sole manner in which you evaluated the property?

A. These are two vacant lots, approximately rectangular in shape, and the only real approach to value that is applicable is what is called the market data approach or sales comparison, wherein you would find similar lots with similar amenities that have recently sold.

Q. Tell me what you did in determining market value?

A. In that—along those lines, I researched what I

thought to be the best comparable, that had the same oceanfront amenities that the subject—because that is the amenity which has the greatest influence on value in this situation.

Page 147

(continued testimony by Donato)

Q. Now, having completed your appraisal of the value in 1988, after studying the situation, did you come to any conclusions about what the value of the property would be now, after passage of the Beachfront Management Act?

A. Well, unfortunately, there is not much precedent for that, Mr. Harness, because we are not too far along from the implementation of the Act to have enough data to tell us exactly what is going to happen.

But it is my opinion that there is some sort of salvage value that can be—that is applicable to this property.

I have used the minimum percentage of ten percent which would relate to fifty-six thousand dollars per lot, and I believe.

Q. What did you derive the ten percent from?

A. Well, I don't really have a good explanation for why that ten percent is there. There is a—one of the things I looked at was some market data.

There is a house that is currently totally within the dead zone out at Edisto Beach that has been for sale for several years. It probably has a market value today of about some sixty thousand dollars. They had an offer on it for twenty thousand dollars.

Obviously, the offer was—that's a far greater percentage than ten percent but it was a buildable structure on there, which the buyer, if he was able to purchase it at twenty thousand dollars, could renovate and live in and take the risk that it would remain there for his lifetime or whatever.

So that ten percent more or less came from that type of information, but I believe the reasons for it are that particularly the climate of knowledge that was available on the date of appraisal which was in June of 1988. We didn't really know what was going to happen with this Beach Front Act. There were several seminars that were put on by different organizations, and the bottom line was that we really don't know what this Act is going to look like until after it is litigated.

So I believe that on the date of the appraisal you have an element there of gambling that a purchaser would be willing to pay a small percentage of the value of that property, hoping there would be some change in the Act that would allow them to use the property.

Number two, there is always the chance that given the —you have erosion, but you also have accretion and there may be accretion that would allow the lines to be moved seaward, also allowing you to use the property.

My third reasoning is that you would have maybe adjoining property owner who would want to purchase the land for control of the land. Although the land is usable today it might not be—it might be usable tomorrow and so consequently without owning the land the adjoining property owner would have no control on it.

Q. Thank you. Answer any questions Mr. Howe might have.

(Howe questioning Donato)

Q. Looking at page 40, where you're talking about this salvage value, you agree that there wasn't any method you followed as far as salvage value is concerned?

A. Correct, Sir.

Q. You say here there's insufficient data to suggest what percentage of value the speculative element might command?

A. Correct.

Q. And is that a true statement?

A. I believe it to be true.

Q. You believe it to be a speculative element?

A. Yes Sir.

Q. Mr. Howe: I'd move to strike his testimony in that regard, Your Honor.

The Court: I would strike the testimony. I understood him to testify to that on direct. He said he had nothing to base the ten percent on except just pure speculation.

Q. I'd like you to look at page 37 of your appraisal.

A. Yes, sir.

Q. The second paragraph. You put in there an analysis of the appreciation of Wild Dunes ocean front lots suggests compounded rates of twenty-four to twenty-five percent per year.

A. Yes, sir.

Q. And you are saying there that your analysis reflects an appreciation of approximately twenty-four to twenty-five percent per year on ocean front lots?

A. Up until 1986.

Q. Now, Lucas held this land for the last year?

A. Yes, sir.

Q. Obviously he couldn't do anything with it?

A. That's correct.

Q. From his prospective, it was valueless?

A. Well, I don't contend that it was valueless.

Q. Listen to my words. I didn't ask you about fair market. From his prospective, the use to which he could put it, it had no value, did it?

A. That's correct.

Q. And in the course of that, he had to pay taxes on it?

A. Yes, sir.

Q. He had to pay regime fees at the Wild Dunes?

A. Yes, sir.

Q. He had a several hundred thousand dollar mortgage on it and he had to pay interest on that, didn't he?

A. Yes.

Q. And in addition to that, whatever figure the Court might determine, there is some difference between what he owed on it and what it's worth in the market place. Let's say he owed Five Hundred thousand Dollars and it was worth a million one or a million two.

That's seven hundred thousand dollars in between and that's equity, isn't it?

A. Correct.

Q. All right. If he had that money he could put it in the bank, couldn't he?

A. Yes, sir.

Q. Get eight or nine percent on that, couldn't he?

A. Yes, sir.

Q. So, he's lost that too.

A. I don't know about that, sir. I'm dealing with June 30, 1988.

Q. I know, but you don't get to get up here and set the perimeters, you know. Let me ask you the question again. If it was marketable in 1986–in 1988, June of 1988, when the Act was passed, he had six or seven hundred thousand dollars in equity, didn't he?

A. If that's what you say he had, yes.

Q. Well, that's a lost opportunity over a year. Don't you call that lost opportunity cost?

A. Yes, sir.

Q. And doesn't that have a value, a simple value just like figuring what he could make on it in the bank?

A. Yes, sir.

Q. Nothing tricky about all that?

A. No, sir.

Q. So as I see it right now, from an appraisal prospective, what we know about this property is
that the man who owns it—whoever owns it gets
to pay taxes on it. Right?

A. Right.

Q. Gets to pay regime fees?

A. Right.

Q. Ought to carry some insurance on that property for liability purposes? That would be a good
idea?

A. Probably not.

Q. You recommend against that.

A. I wouldn't insure my lot, no, sir.

Q. And he's certainly got to pay the mortgage?

A. Yes, sir.

Q. And other than that, that's about all he can do
with it, isn't it?

A. Yes, sir.

Q, Thank you, sir.

Redirect Examination by Mr. Harness:

Q. In your experience as an appraiser, is it your opinion this lot has value today.

A. Yes, sir. I believe it has value.

Q. Nothing further.

Mr. Harness: Your Honor that's the State's case.

Mr. Smith: Nothing further from the plaintiff.

Mr. Howe: Your Honor, I'd like to let the Court set the tone in a non-jury action as to—some judges look at you and say, you don't propose to make a speech to us, do you, Mr. Howe. I mean, we will handle that any way you want to do it. Needless to say, both of us will be glad to talk with you and give you our view but on the other hand if you think you've got a pretty good feel for the case we'll leave that up to you.

Mr. Harness: If it please the Court, I think our position is clear and I don't think I can articulate any more than what you know. I would suggest to the Court it might be appropriate for us to just submit proposed Orders or additional briefs.

The Court: What was the State's responsibility if that house washed away?

Mr. Harness: The State had no responsibility— the State or the Coastal Council had no responsibility but—

The Court: You all are just interested in preserving the beaches?

Mr. Harness: Preserving the beaches and now we've been charged with responsibility to be certain beach front property is sited so that people aren't threatened by hurricanes or tidal erosion. So it gives us a double role now.

Prior to that what we were trying to do was to protect critical areas from ill-planned development🖉 and that's the — the lines did not allow the State to do that and that's the reason the Act was passed.

Your Honor, if it's any help to you, what I've done — I think Mr. Smith would agree. I put together the 1977 Beach Front Management Act and the 1988 Act, and the administrative interpretation that got us here today in a booklet for you for your review. It might be of some help.

The Court: Mr. Harness, there is no provision like applications to grant variances or anything like that?

Mr. Harness: Your Honor, one of the difficulties that we are facing is that the Legislature did not do that. They did provide for remedy if you've got an existing structure that was destroyed by storm, in terms of what a Judge can do.

🖉 If you are swayed by this argument, turn to page 252 and read about the hypocritical actions taken by the state when *their* money was at risk. —D.L.

Really what it does is put variance remedy in the hands of the Court, to say that, all right, gentlemen, if you're not going to pay damages, I want you to allow him to build something on this lot, and what I'm allowed - - when the Judge tells me that I should, I go back to my Council and say, listen, we lost the fight; you ought to issue a permit and go on down the road.

Of course, that's a very unpleasant way to do variance—make it responsibility of the court—but the Legislature has not seen fit to give us any way of working out the problem.

The Court: Your comment at the beginning of the case was: he just bought a pig in a poke and that's the way it was.

Mr.Harness: Your Honor, I think I did say that. One of the things—let me put that in proper context.

The Court: You can't put that in context in this case. That's an awful big price to pay, nine hundred and seventy-five thousand dollars.

Mr. Harness: I agree with that comment, Your Honor.

The Court: And he doesn't look like the kind of person that—it's an awful big investment just to absolutely lose it overnight. Isn't it?

Mr. Harness: Your Honor, it's a tremendous investment to lose overnight and I agree. The point we're trying to make from the State's point of view is: the Act has been passed and prohibits construction that may end up creating the problems we discussed.

It's a technical conflict between the public interests and the private right to use property unencumbered. ✎

I don't know what the answers are but that's our position.

The Court: What's the public interest here when you have an accretion of a long period of time and you're going to prohibit him from using his property? Your own witnesses testified over the long haul it's going to continue to expand.

Mr. Harness: Your Honor, maybe I didn't do my job right here today, but I hope Your Honor would see the area, while it is generally accreting, is subject to periodic events of erosion because of the character of the area.

We've stipulated to the fact that it is overall an accretion.

It's not like a steady straight-up line.

The Court: All right. Well, I'll think about it overnight, gentlemen.

On each side, people built as they wished... but the government said, "no, you cannot use *your* property as you want."

5

Judge Toal's Revenge

OR:

Gloom, Despair, and Agony On Me

We left the courthouse that summer day in August of 1989 feeling pretty good. The state had failed, in my opinion and in Ellison and Gedney's opinion, to prove any of the things that they had set out to prove. In fact, they had helped to prove our case with their own witnesses. Cotton Harness had even asked the court on a couple of instances to do exactly what we had asked; pay us for the land that the "harsh" action of the South Carolina General Assembly had rendered valueless.

The state had said that the law was needed for mostly scenic purposes to promote tourism. This is South Carolina's largest industry by far, along the coast. They wanted to allow natural process to occur. I guess mankind is not natural in their view.

This, of course, was a new doctrine articulated in the form of the Beachfront Management Act. As to the danger of houses washing into other houses, recent experiences with hurricanes, Hugo and Andrew, clearly show that houses built to hurricane standards of construction can withstand storms very well, even on the front beach in the direct path of a raging storm at its worst. Damage inland from those two monster hurricanes was just as bad, if not worse, than damage to houses directly on the open beachfront.

The hundreds of millions of dollars that were lost, were not lost exclusively on the beachfront. The great majority of the losses occurred off the front beach area where these so-called experts would have you believe it was safer to build. (Raymon Finch always reminds me that an "expert" is a man who can tell you a hundred ways to make love, but doesn't know any women). And these arguments by the state had nothing to do with the case, because we had not challenged the purpose behind the act, as I explained in the last chapter.

To do that we would have had to use the "due process" part of the Fifth Amendment and we felt that it was a useless argument to make in today's legal environment. Besides, the "Just Compensation" clause was where the rubber meets the road.

The state had tried to use two basic arguments to avoid paying. The first was that the lots were never suitable to build on, and we had shot that down easily. Even their own witnesses stated that, but for the Beachfront Management Act, there was nothing to keep me from building. The other argument was that there was salvage value left in the lots of fifty six-thousand dollars each. The appraiser admitted that he had pulled those numbers out of the air. I guess everyone is entitled to his opinion. Some people still believe in the tooth fairy. I hope the state paid the man well for that performance. I remember that he even did it with a straight face although he did blush a bit from time to time when he said he had no backup data for his claim.

On the other hand, our witness, Don Pardue had good data to backup his assertions of value. As to the claim that a neighbor might pay for something he already had for free, Judge Patterson's response said it all.

I knew that we had won the argument. Now we had to see if the judge felt the same way. Judge Patterson didn't waste time. His ruling came out ten days after we had argued the case, on August 14, 1989. He ruled in our favor, saying there had indeed been a taking compensable under both the

United States Constitution and the state of South Carolina's constitution. He ordered the state to pay me $1,232,387.50 as just compensation. I, in return, had to deed the lots over to the state. What a relief! I had my day in court and had been granted a just verdict. Had the matter ended there, it would have been just compensation. The Judge had even made the statement that the opinion was so tight that he didn't see a problem with the expected appeal by the state. He was right on the law and wrong on the politics.

I thought that the year-long ordeal for me, my family and my bankers was almost over. In fact, Judge Paherson's ruling had waved a red flag under the noses of the environmentalists nationwide. But he had particularly upset one dedicated environmentalist who was in a position to do something about it. That person was the newly appointed South Carolina Supreme Court Justice, Jean Toal.

She was the most recently elected member to the South Carolina Supreme Court and she was up to bat on this case next. The South Carolina Coastal Council appealed Judge Paterson's decision as expected.

The appeal went directly to the South Carolina Supreme Court without stopping at any interim appeal level. My attorneys were confident. There had been no serious problems with the case on the lower level. Cotton Harness, the lawyer for the state, had even asked the judge to rule the way he did during the course of the trial. The ruling from the judge was legally, a good solid opinion. It was to be a routine appeal that both sides felt we would win. But we had not reckoned with the resourcefulness of Justice Toal.

I asked my lawyers if I needed to be present when they argued the case, but neither Gedney nor Ellison thought that it was necessary. With complete confidence in the outcome, Ellison and Gedney argued the appeal in South Carolina Supreme Court on April 2, 1990.

The arguments had gone well, I was told. The questions asked by the justices were basically along the same lines as the ones raised in Judge Patterson's court. Gedney and Ellison were of the opinion that the issue would soon be resolved in our favor. The South Carolina Supreme Court now had the matter under advisement.

South Carolina's Supreme Court is made up of five justices. They are elected by the General Assembly of South Carolina. The justices serve until they reach the mandatory retirement age of seventy-two. Most of the members of the General Assembly are lawyers. Most of the justices who sit on the Supreme court are lawyers. A lot of them are elected right out of the General Assembly. Justice Toal had been a very active and vocal member of the General Assembly.

I was familiar with her name because in the past she had been very much a liberal activist and had gained a lot of public attention from the press because of her outspoken positions. I had not followed her career closely, however, and was only vaguely aware that she was now sitting on the Supreme Court. I had heard the rumor that her opponents in the legislature had elected her to move her out of the General Assembly. She was a tough adversary, and so they kicked her upstairs, so to speak. Thanks a lot ! May your lives become as interesting as mine.

Unknowingly, I had scorned her work from her previous incarnation as a General Assembly Person. It was only after the appeal decision was rendered by the South Carolina Supreme Court that I was made aware of the fact that one of her projects, while a member of the General Assembly, was the passage of, you guessed it, the 1988 Beachfront Management Act!

I was told that she had been instrumental in the composition of the bill and in the floor management of its passage. She had of course, voted in favor of the bill in 1988 and was now being called upon to decide whether what she did in 1988 was constitutional. Had I been aware of this political tie-in, I would have asked for her to excuse herself from this case.

I wasn't aware of this until it was too late to

make a difference. Gedney and Ellison were aware of this fact, but she was only one vote in five. There was no law that said she would have to disqualify herself even if we had asked her to. There is, in fact, a United States Supreme Court decision that says this kind of conflict of interest is not grounds for dismissal. They felt confident that the other members could handle this and reach a favorable decision. They were wrong.

Never underestimate a person who has been elected to office, been a political activist, believes passionately in the justness of her causes, and is so tough politically that the only way to handle her is to elect her to a higher office. To give Justice Toal her due, I just wish that she had been on my side in this fight. She was a determined opponent.

Time passed and the court had not ruled. I would call either Gedney or Ellison every two or three weeks and at first the answers were the same. They said the arguments had gone well and that we should expect a ruling very soon. They also said for me not to worry so much.

As time passed, I began to feel uneasy and sensed too, that my attorneys were not as confident as before. After three or four months of waiting, the rumor mills started. I had some supposedly well-placed friends that knew someone, who knew someone, who knew one of the judges. They had reportedly asked about the case and knew when a verdict was coming. I was told that we had won three votes to two. I had asked Gedney about every new bit of leaked information. He always told me to discount such rumors.

On my next biweekly call to Gedney, I got an ominous answer to my question of "have you heard anything yet." He surprised me by saying that he had heard a new rumor. It was the opposite vote count. Reliable sources had told Gedney that it was three to two against us.

The issue was being hotly debated by the justices and we seemed to be losing. I became a little nervous when I heard that the vote was so close in our favor. When Gedney, who is very well connected in the state passed on the rumor that we were now losing, I was stunned. How, I asked, could a case this cut and dried, and this well presented be in trouble? Couldn't those people read plain English? Evidently, three of them seemed to need a remedial course on the Constitution.

It was January of 1991 and still no ruling. Almost a year had passed since the appeal had been argued in front of the South Carolina Supreme Court. What the hell was going on? While we were waiting for word from the South Carolina Supreme Court, the General Assembly had been back in action. Since we had filed our lawsuit, additional suits had also been filed in federal court. Other landowners who were affected like me by this law were only awaiting the outcome of my case to file their suits. The pressure was mounting on the state to lessen the harshness of this draconian law.

It wasn't popular pressure coming from the public, but it was pressure from affected landowners threatening to go to court. The potential liability to the state was beginning to mount up. If we won our suit, then some serious money was going to have to be paid to a lot of other people, as well. The taxpayers were getting uneasy and that made the General Assembly members nervous. When the bill was debated, no one had talked about contingent liabilities. In their rush to be politically correct, they had overlooked that basic issue.

The lawsuits that had been filed, the law suits threatened and the plain unfairness of the law had prompted our General Assembly to pass an amendment to the 1988 law. This new act was called the 1990 Amendment to the 1988 Beachfront Management Act. It was a small step in the right direction, but by no means did it repeal the ill-conceived law.

This new amendment allowed the coastal council to issue "special" permits for construction in the forbidden zones. First, they had to take down the barbed wire, the guard towers, and muzzle the attack dogs. When the shoot-to-kill order was rescinded, I felt that we were making progress. That's exaggerated a little, but it was how I felt.

There were real landmines, however, in this 1990 amendment. First of all, restrictions were put on the square footage that you were allowed to build. I never have understood the reasoning behind that. What difference does it make? The value of a home is not necessarily tied to the size. One of the arguments used to justify this restriction was the cost of replacement. However, the law stated that if more than fifty percent of your home needed to be replaced, it would be prohibited by law. You could not rebuild.

The other "special" part of these new permits was, that if the coastal council decided the beach had become active again, then they could force the individual homeowner to tear down his home. The people who determined what constituted an active beach were the bureaucrats at the Coastal Council. The definition of "active" was to be whatever they said it was. How's that for flexibility? It certainly gave me that warm and fuzzy feeling in the pit of my stomach knowing that those beaureaucrats would take care of me and my property.

Just trust me, the amended law said; let the beaureaucrats decide what's good for you. They already had the power to redraw the original line every five years. But under the "special" permit, they didn't have to wait five years to harass the property owner. They could begin by just writing up a new definition of what an active beach was. If they found, in their vast expert wisdom, that you were in the way of reverse progress (erosion or mother nature, as the case may be), then off with your home.

In effect, the coastal council was setting up the newly permitted beachfront homeowner. If you agreed to accept the special permit, then you had, in fact, agreed to the special conditions of that permit. Now they're counting on the courts to say that by accepting the special permit, you have agreed to the terms and conditions written therein (I guess government is the only one who can change the rules as it goes along). The next time they act, individuals would lose not only land, but homes as well. And this time around, the property owner will not have the benefit of saying that the government changed the rules and therefore must pay compensation.

Another portion of the 1990 amendment said that all present litigation was unaffected by the new amendment. This curious language meant that the state was not allowing me to take advantage of the new amendment, even if I had wanted to. I was locked in and would have to see how this played out. Of course, the public has never been made aware of this. The state was to keep silent about this little known fact throughout the coming fight, and even to use it against me, both in court and in the publicity war that was soon to be launched by the state and the environmental lobby. They tried to mark me as the greedy developer who was trying to rip off the state, because I wouldn't try to get a "special permit."

The language pertaining to this restriction was pretty straight forward. The exact wording is presented below.

Section 8 of the 1990 Act No. 607, effective June 25, 1990, provides as follows;

Except as otherwise specifically provided in this act, the provisions of this act shall be applied only prospectively and shall not affect any legal action commenced or any cause of action occurring as a result of an event or events which occurred before the effective date of this act. Any such action must be governed by the provisions of Section 48-39-10 through 48-39-360, as amended by act 634 of 1988, and in existence before the effective date of this act.

As the reader can see from the language above, I was in this until the fat lady sang. I was hoping that she would be singing my song and not the one that goes " this land is my land, this land is your land." I was hoping that in the end, it would be my land only. Mine, and the bank's and the attorneys', that is.

Finally, on February 11, 1991, after almost a year of deliberation, the ruling came down from the Supreme Court. Judge Jean Toal, writing for the majority in a split three to two opinion, as follows:

DAVID LUCAS

David H. Lucas, Respondent.

V.

South Carolina Coastal

Council, Appellant.

No.23342

Supreme Court of South Carolina.

Heard April 2, 1990.

Decided Feb. 11, 1991.

Owner of beachfront property brought action alleging that application of the Beachfront Management Act to his property constituted a taking without just compensation. The Common Pleas Court of Charleston County, Larry R. Paterson, Special J., awarded landowner damages and appeal was taken. The Supreme Court, Toal J., held that governmental regulation of use of landowner's property, in order to prevent serious public harm☜, did not amount to a "regulatory taking" of property for which compensation was required.

Reversed.

Harwell, J., Filed dissenting opinion in which Chandler, J., concurred.

I agreed with all but two words; not and reversed. As incredible as it seemed to me at the

☜ If you are swayed by this argument, turn to page 252 and read about the hypocritical actions taken by the state when *their* money was at risk. —D.L.

time, I had lost. And, I had lost in South Carolina. In South Carolina, supposedly, one of the most conservative states in the union. Private property had been taken without paying for it and this had been sanctioned by both the legislature and now the watchdog of the people's rights: the South Carolina Supreme Court.

It took me a few days to digest the ruling that Judge Toal had come up with to justify her political views. She did it in spite of both the United States Constitution and the South Carolina State Constitution. I will try to highlight this most dangerous of rulings; a ruling that had been presented as a decision to protect the environment. But what, in effect, it really did was threaten to undermine our freedoms and turn us into a police state with no real guarantees for our property or security.

I hope that you will be as frightened by this way of thinking as I have been, since I realized that there are people in power who will use it to further their political views, in spite of oaths to uphold and protect the Constitution. Here, in part, is what she wrote. I have once again presented a condensed version of what was written.

Toal, Justice:

This appeal concerns whether the enforcement and application of the 1988 Beachfront

Management Act to the plaintiff-respondent's property is a taking of such property without just compensation.

LAW/ANALYSIS

[1] Although the regulatory takings question is a complex one, this appeal is in our view a relatively straightforward one. The issue is whether governmental regulation of the use of property👎, in order to prevent serious public harm, amounts to a "regulatory taking" of property for which compensation must be paid.

[2] Lucas concedes that the Beachfront Management Act is properly and validly designed to preserve the extremely valuable resource which is South Carolina's beaches. He concedes that the preservation of this existing public resource from harm is a "laudable goal.." He admittedly fails to attack the validity of the legislative declaration of its "findings" and "policy" embodied in Sections 1 and 2 of 1988 Act No. 634. The Court is therefore in no position to question the legislative scheme or purpose👎. (Here is where the court abandons the due process part of the Fifth Amendment.)

(I, in fact, conceded nothing about whether the act is needed. She just wrote it into her ruling as

---

👎 If you are swayed by this argument, turn to page 252 and read about the hypocritical actions taken by the state when *their* money was at risk. —D.L.

a form of justification. This question never came up in our original trial.)

> [3] By failing to contest these legislative findings, Lucas concedes that the beach/dune area of South Carolina's shores is an extremely valuable public resource; and that discouraging new construction in close proximity to the beach/dune area is necessary to prevent a great public harm. 👎

(This is all wishful thinking conjured up by a proponent of the law to justify disregarding the constitution. I was never asked about what I thought of the bill. I conceded nothing of the sort).

> Lucas maintains that if a regulation operates to deprive a land owner of "all economically viable use" of his property, it has worked a "taking" for which compensation is due, regardless of any other consideration. This is simply an erroneous statement of existing law.

(This is a true statement about the taking part, Justice Toal's statement of the law was the erroneous statement of existing law, not mine. But how would we be allowed to prove it?)

I will not bore the reader with the entire tortured decision that she concocted. It was long and wrong. She ended her opinion with the following:

Lucas's defacto concession of the legislative

scheme and of its purposes🖐 makes the instant set of facts appropriate for the application of the "Mugler" rule. We need not address the remaining issues in this case, and we express no opinion regarding them. Accordingly we reverse the decision of the lower court.

Gregory,C.J., and FINNEY,J., concur. HARWELL, and CHANDLER, JJ., dissent in separate opinion.

What the hell was she talking about? I had a simple case and who was this guy Mugler she was bringing up? All of a sudden my simple case wasn't so simple anymore. I had just been *Muglered.* I had just had my initiation into the fantastic world of legal reasoning. I was no longer a trusting virgin. After reading this concoction, my belief in our judicial system was severely strained and about to be severely tested. I was to be educated in the wild and wacky ways of the United States legal system. I had always thought that the law was the law. It ain't so. The law is whatever the judge says it is. Black becomes blue and vise versa. I was both black and blue. Thanks a lot, Jean baby!

The "Mugler" case mentioned above is from a case that happened in Kansas. It is also from the last century. Now, there is nothing wrong with using an old case. After all, the constitution is over two hundred years old. But this case had to do with prohibition in Kansas, another popular issue that was emotionally charged. It was the "environmentalism" of its day. When the courts bowed to popular political pressures then, as the South Carolina Court had just done, they had damaged the integrity of the Constitution in America.

The Mugler case concerned the use of the police powers of the state of Kansas that were used to regulate the making of whiskey. Actually, it outlawed the making of whiskey and provided no compensation to the owner of a distillery. This guy's name was Mugler and he lost a United States Supreme court decision way back in 1887. Here is an explanation of Mugler written in the dissent of Judge Harwell:

"At issue in " Mugler" was a statue prohibiting use of a distillery for the manufacture of intoxicating liquors. The Supreme Court upheld the statue and reasoned that the power of the state to prohibit uses of property "prejudicial to the health, morals, or the public safety of the public, is not... burdened with the condition that the state must compensate such individual owners for pecuniary losses they may sustain."

Mugler stands for the proposition that where the legislature has deemed an act to be necessary for the public's health, safety, and welfare, the judiciary need not scrutinize the acts of the legislature, regardless of the loss suffered by the property owner. A prohibition on the use of property, enacted in the interest of the community as a whole, the Mugler court held, cannot be deemed a taking or appropriation."

Justice Harwell goes on to say that the court has changed that law and now says that, "The two factors that the court considers relevant, have become integral parts of our takings analysis. We have held that land use regulation can effect a taking if it 'does not substantially advance legitimate state interest... or denies an owner economically viable use of his land.'"

The arguments among the justices came down to this: Justice Toal and a majority of the court felt that by building a home on my lots, I was, under the new law, endangering the public. I was endangering the public because the new 1988 Beachfront Management Act said so. And that was reason enough in their opinion to allow the state to use its police powers to steal my property. Since I had not challenged the reasons behind the act, the Court would not do it for me. And since the state had used its legitimate police powers to regulate a nuisance, it owed me nothing. Harwell disagreed. He said that "the law was not to regulate a nuisance, but to primarily promote ascetic goals beneficial to all, but not to regulate a nuisance."

Again Justice Harwell speaks in his dissent. "In my opinion the Beachfront Management Act does not have as its primary purpose the prevention of a nuisance, and is therefore not subject to the Mugler analysis. The activities and effects the Act seeks to prohibit do not rise to such a level as to be considered "noxious." The primary purpose of the Beachfront Management System is to protect and foster the regeneration of the beach/dune system, the benefits of which enure to the State of South Carolina by, among other things, promoting tourism, creating a habitat for indigenous flora and fauna, creating a place which harbors natural beauty, and providing a barrier and buffer from high tides, storm surge, hurricanes and normal erosion...

"Upon my review of the Act, I conclude that none of these intended purposes can fairly be said to resemble a nuisance...

"Accordingly, I do not find that the Act at issue here seeks to further 'public interest in preventing activities similar to public nuisances' such that it is entitled to the protection afforded by Mugler." (The protection he mentions is that the state under Mugler would not have to pay compensation).

(Now he addresses the loss of economically viable use). "The lots now lack fair market value and there is no economically viable use..., I find the valuation of Coastal Council's expert to have been totally speculative. Accordingly, since Lucas's land has no fair market value, I would hold that the second part of the test, deprival of economically viable use, has been met and a taking established."

I was dumbfounded that Harwell had not carried the day. I read Justice Toal's unfair opinion over and over. This did not make sense to me. If the Legislature could muster up a majority, then it could pass any law it wanted to and there was nothing this court would do to stop it, even if the act was unconstitutional. What had happened to the Bill of Rights? What about the guarantees of the South Carolina Constitution? Did none of this matter to these people? Ironically, as things turned out, without her help in the form of this ultra biased ruling, we would have not had such a great case to promote the cause of private property rights. The Lord works in mysterious ways.

This was really not a new issue. It was as old as civilized society itself. The Bill of Rights has been constantly under attack throughout our history. I had been guilty of seeing only what I wanted to see in the constitution. On some issues, I had mentally backed unconstitutional acts when I had agreed with the political reasons for doing them. I had been just as guilty in principle as anyone else. Isn't there a saying about whose ox is getting gored?

The entire Civil Rights Movement had been about the individual's rights. The American Revolution was about the rights of the American colonist; the Magna Carta was about the rights of Englishmen. The War Between the States was about rights. All of these tumultuous events were over diverse interpretations of the rights of individuals. This was over more than money and land. This was about freedom. This was about the American dream. This was about the long journey towards the perfection of the natural rights of man.

I thought about all of those who had sacrificed so much for this country. I could do no less. Fight this attack on my constitutional rights I must, and I would. It was the least that I could do, considering how much good fortune America's liberties had so recently and generously given to me. The continuing fight for freedoms in America had gotten close to home. My duty was to continue that fight in this judicial arena. The ancient struggle to secure property rights for all men, not just a privileged few, was about to have a new dedicated warrior. Let the games continue.

6
The Long Wait

OR:

You Don't Have To Die Or Be Catholic to Go To Purgatory

I was fired up. This was not right; morally or legally. I certainly couldn't afford to roll over and play dead on a million dollar investment. I believed that I had understanding bankers, but they were still bankers. Their understanding was that they got paid and sooner, rather than later. If I couldn't pay then, I was no longer going to be issued a preferred visa gold card. I would no longer get calls from their investment counselors and would be taken off of their promotional mailing lists. It would be better all around if we took this thing as far as we could and won. I called Gedney to set up a strategy session. Then a funny thing happened on the way to the United States Supreme Court. Somehow, I lost my two lawyers. How do you lose lawyers, especially two characters like Gedney and Ellison?

We met soon after the opinion came down. We had thirty days to appeal the decision. Gedney was, I think, more depressed about the loss than I was. He wasn't confident about our chances on appeal. This appeal would go directly to the Supreme Court of the United States.

I thought there were several other appeals courts to go through, but Gedney assured me that it was hard enough having only one court to appeal to, and actually, it was better because it would be less expensive than going to other courts. In my anger and indignation over the outcome in the South Carolina Supreme Court, and my subsequent ardor to continue to fight this injustice, I had not thought about the expense. My lawyers had not forgotten that little item, however.

I was somewhat taken aback by the thought of going to the highest court in the land so quickly. Gedney explained that other than the United States Supreme Court, there was no court higher than a State Supreme Court.

The main problem was that less than one in ten appeals are even heard by the Court. The most difficult part is to be granted "certiorari," or the right to be heard. The lawyers shorten this to say that one has been granted "cert." After you are granted cert, additional briefs are filed. These are also expensive. If, after reading the briefs, the United States Supreme Court wants to hear your case, then it is off to Washington to make your argument.

The odds of ever being heard were indeed long. Another source was more pessimistic; he said that only four percent of the cases sent up to the United States Supreme Court are accepted. That kind of talk certainly was discouraging. I asked Gedney if he or Ellison had ever argued before the Supreme Court. The answer was no. It was something that most attorneys never get a chance to do in their careers. Its like playing in the Super Bowl or pitching in the World Series. Many people play the game, but only a very few ever get to the top. In the case of the Supreme Court, the odds just weren't good.

Gedney also explained that the case had moved into constitutional law. This was not his field of expertise. Gedney was a trial lawyer and this was going to take a lot of research. Since his was a small firm, it would be expensive for him to take time away from pending cases and commit to my case full time without a generous retainer. Gedney mentioned the amount he had in mind, and I told him that I would get back to him after thinking it over for a few days. I contacted Ellison. He and I met to discuss his views on what to do next.

Ellison was really upset with Judge Toal's decision. The construction of our case and the decision not to attack the Beachfront Management

Act on constitutional grounds had been his. On his recommendation we had disregarded the background of the law and asked directly for compensation. He felt that Judge Toal's decision was a slap in the face to him personally and professionally. I said something to the effect that it was my money that she had slapped him with, but that didn't seem to cheer him up very much.

Ellison didn't have much to add to what Gedney had told me. His firm was even smaller than Gedney's at the time and he felt it would be best to go with a larger firm. I needed a firm that had a special interest in this kind of constitutional question. They would have more time, people and financial resources to commit to the job. If I could find someone with experience to argue in front of the Supreme Court, that would be the best solution for me. I knew they were giving me good advice.

It was clear that I was going to need to find new attorneys. Gedney and Ellison had done a good job up until this point, but now, it was up to me to keep the ball rolling. This was almost as bad as the day I got the South Carolina Supreme Court's decision. Not only had I lost the suit, but unless I could come up with a large retainer, I would also lose my attorneys. Gedney provided me with the names of some lawyers who had called expressing an interest in my case. I decided to call them before I responded in the negative to

Gedney's proposal.

There were two or three letters from interested law firms. I contacted a professor of constitutional law, David Bederman. He was enthusiastic and sympathetic, but not able to handle the case on his own. He did, however, offer to become part of a legal team if I was successful in putting such a team together. Then I followed up with a call to the Pacific Legal Defense Fund. They had been defending property rights out on the west coast for a long time and had also argued cases before the United States Supreme Court.

I spoke to their representative, an attorney named Tim Suni. He listened to my predicament and told me that he would talk to his board of directors to see if they could help. They had been involved in the "takings" issues for quite some time and had not only argued, but won cases before the Supreme Court on property rights. I was impressed with their background.

Back in 1989, I had hired another attorney in Columbia to handle a business deal that had gone bad. This legal fight was a big case involving millions of dollars. I had interviewed several firms in the state and had hired the Finkel Firm in Columbia. My sister, April, who is an attorney with the McNair Firm in the same city, had helped with the interviews.

We had considered using my sister's firm, but

they represented the banks that had the money at risk and there was too much of a conflict of interest. Jerry Finkel had been impressive during that first meeting. He had grasped the essence of my story immediately and had moved ahead rapidly with the case.

Jerry confirmed our appeal to the United States Supreme Court was an expensive and difficult undertaking. He understood perfectly well the reluctance on the part of the other two lawyers to continue with the case under the circumstances. His was a larger firm than Gedney's or Ellison's and he was very interested in constitutional law.

As a matter of fact, Jerry is a part-time professor at the University of South Carolina Law School. He said that he was interested in handling this case for me. I was surprised, because to my knowledge his firm didn't do contingency work. I had made it perfectly clear that was what I needed. Under a contingency arrangement, the lawyers only got paid if they won.

The real estate industry was on the ropes and nothing that I was doing looked promising. Since I was, by this time, out of cash, I could not afford to pay even a small retainer. Jerry had never argued before the Supreme Court, but it was something that he had always dreamed of doing. I told him to hold on, that he might soon get his chance.

Later that same day, I met with Camden Lewis. I had known "Camy" since my days as a football player at the University of South Carolina. Camy had played quarterback for Army under coach Paul Deitzel. He would have been famous, but the quarterback for Navy at the time had stolen all of the service academy's publicity. As a matter of fact, he stole most of the other colleges' publicity as well. His name was Roger Staubach. Camy had come with Coach Deitzel, after graduating from West Point, to Carolina and as a graduate assistant coach. This was at the same time I played defensive end for the Gamecocks. He had coached the scout squads and attended law school. After graduation, he had gone to work at the South Carolina Attorney General's office. He had been assigned the task of prosecuting other attorneys for malpractice. This had not endeared him to other attorneys in South Carolina, but it proved that he had courage, determination and a thick skin. These were qualities that I knew would serve me well in this case.

After a few years with the State, Camy started his own firm. He had done well with his practice during the intervening years and had built a solid reputation as a tough, trial lawyer. As things turned out, he knew Jerry Finkel very well. They had even collaborated on a few cases.

Columbia is loaded with attorneys. The law

school at the University of South Carolina turns out hundreds of them every year. Still, with all those lawyers, I needed a seasoned veteran. Camy had argued a case in front of the United States Supreme Court a couple of years before.

I asked how it had turned out and he told me that he had lost. Well, I figured that an unsatisfactory experience is some times better than no experience and the price was right. Camy and I called Jerry to discuss their potential collaboration and involvement in my property rights case. I told them of David Bederman's interest and they decided to talk it over with him and get back to me.

I returned to Charleston feeling a little better. Earlier, I had felt alone and abandoned. My options were limited because of my financial difficulties. But, if I could put together a good team, then this case might have a chance of moving forward.

A few days passed and the Pacific Legal Defense Fund called from California. Their board of directors had voted to allow their staff to take the case. They were cautiously optimistic about our chances because of the last few property rights rulings of the Supreme Court. They had studied the South Carolina Supreme Court decision and sensed that we had a better than even shot.

The issues in my case were so clear, that they

felt this was a good case to push. They offered to take the case for expenses. At the time, I couldn't even afford that generous offer. I was aware that they had won a Supreme Court case called the "Nolan" case, but at the time I didn't realize the significance of that victory in the property rights wars. I thanked them and told them I would sleep on it and get back with them. They didn't realize just how bad my finances were at the time.

Later that week, Jerry called and asked me to come to Columbia. The following morning, I got into my car and made the two-and-a-half hour drive from Charleston. Jerry and Camy began our meeting by telling me that in their opinion we had a better than average chance of being heard. That was the good news.

Then they changed tactics and started talking about all of the difficulties they would encounter along the way. I knew from experience that this was the fee negotiating phase. They must have a course in law school called Fee Negotiation 101. Each time that I have ever worked with lawyers, this is exactly the same tactic that is used.

First they tell you what a good case you have, to build up your confidence in their abilities. They show off that legal education and tell the client how he has been wronged. That builds up your hopes and your confidence in your chances of winning. After you are sufficiently hooked, they subtly change tactics. The conversation now turns to talk about the difficulties of the case, the court expenses that must be absorbed, the long hours needed to properly prepare, and the time that your case will take away from their paying clients. All of this sets you up for the discussion of their fee. As I had expected, they asked for a contingency fee of one third, plus expenses. The lawyers from the Pacific Legal Fund had offered a better deal, but I wasn't in a very strong bargaining position.

Besides, even being granted "cert" was a long way off, very uncertain and they were extending me credit at a time when I really needed it. No one else had come forward with an offer of help. Even my bank who knew perfectly well of my financial difficulties and stood to lose millions of dollars both on my lots and other properties on the coast offered no financial help with the legal expenses.

These two guys, along with David Bederman, had stepped up to the plate and I was grateful. For whatever personal motives, be it fame, fortune, philosophy or friendship, they had decided to take the case. In reality, I had nowhere else to go, so I agreed to their terms. They had signed up Professor David Bederman to do constitutional research work. He had just moved to Emory University in Atlanta and would work from there.

The die had been cast. I had managed to pull

together a team of good lawyers. They had agreed to a contingency fee arrangement and had even agreed to front the expenses. The one third plus expenses was high, but given the circumstances and the lack of support from any other quarter, it was a fair deal. After fretting over the future of this case and this issue, it looked as if I would be able to stay in the fight at least for awhile longer.

Judge Toal had struck a strong blow for the idea of a police state. I was blocked by her action. I had an old football coach, C.E. Teal, way back in grammar school in Bishopville, South Carolina, who used to tell me over and over again: "Son, it's not a sin to get blocked, but it is a sin to stay blocked."

I didn't intend to stay blocked, legally, financially, or politically. This was something that I was determined to see through until the last whistle. All of my perseverance was not enough to speed up the wheels of justice, however. I had heard that the wheels of justice turn slowly, and although the first trial under Judge Paterson, had moved quickly, the South Carolina Supreme Court had given me a portent of things to come. It had taken over a year to prepare the case, argue the appeal, and another year to get an answer. After my legal team prepared its appeal to the United States Supreme Court and submitted it to Washington, all that we could do was wait. I wondered if those wheels were moving at all.

That is a helpless feeling. You find that you call your attorneys and discuss the arguments with them over and over. The only good thing about the wait was that I really began to understand the law. I received an intense education in "takings law." I read everything that my attorneys read. I poured over case law after case law. Soon I began to see the problem.

7

The Cavalry to the Rescue... Sorta

OR:

The Good Guys and Gals Now wear Those Black Robes Don't They?

My finances had continued to deteriorate. The real estate that I had invested in during the 1980s had dropped in value along with real estate all over the country. Income properties that were performing well did not have ready buyers. The market was flooded with land for sale. I was forced by my bank to sell properties at a deep discount just to keep them from pulling the rug out from under me and forcing me into bankruptcy. They wanted to be paid and paid now.

In one instance, a piece of ocean front property that had been worth 1.5 million dollars in a good market was sold for two hundred thousand cash. That cash was pledged to the bank. When I was fortunate enough to sell a property, the most difficult task was convincing the bank to let me keep some money to continue to operate and pursue the two lawsuits. It was truly a humiliating experience. The irony was that the bank stood to lose much more than I did, through the taking of property without compensation. I could not understand why they wanted to fight me at every turn instead of offering to help me.

I was, in reality, defending their interests as well as my own. Since they were one of the top ten banks in the United States, they had hundreds of millions of dollars directly at risk in coastal property alone. If I lost the fight and arbitrary police powers were allowed to rule over the Bill of Rights, then a lot of their assets would be in jeopardy.

Instead of helping me, all that I got was obstruction. They forced me to liquidate my hard earned wealth at a great discount to make partial payments on the past due loans. As time wore on, they even made the statement that they thought I was going to lose and that continuing was pointless. I was appalled at the lack of foresight shown by this bank.

All that mattered to them was today and their

present loan portfolio. They allowed me just enough room to inch forward. In this case, if it had been left up to the bankers, they would have taken all that I had, bankrupted me, and walked away from the fight. This would have exposed their stockholders and every other property owner and mortgage holder in the United States to the same kind of governmental theft of assets to which I had been subjected. If a clear-cut case like mine failed, then no one else had any chance to protect their property. This did not seem to matter. In fact, they turned my account over to their collection agency and I was no longer allowed to deal directly with the bank.

One day in January of 1992, I was having one of my sessions with the collection agency. They had grown even more impatient. It had been months since we had filed our request to be heard in United States Supreme Court and had not received an answer.

The collection agency was in the process of denying my request to keep some funds after I was forced into another fire sale of my property. They had agreed, in writing when this case began, to allow me to keep enough assets to see this legal process through. I was facing bankruptcy if they didn't relent and live up to our agreement. I could always sue them, but the last thing that I wanted or needed was another lawsuit.

This time they were insisting on taking all of the money from the property sale. The situation was serious and I was using every bargaining skill that I possessed when I got a telephone call from the *Charlotte Observer*, a North Carolina newspaper. The reporter asked me to comment on how I felt about being granted a hearing before the United States Supreme Court.

I was stunned at first. I had been fighting so long and hard without any good news that I thought this must be a mistake or a false alarm. The collection agents were convinced I would be denied my day in court and we had just been arguing about what to do when the call came through.

I dialed Finkel's number. He had received similar calls and verified the reporters' statement that the Supreme Court of the United States of America had granted a writ of certiorari to the plaintiff in the case of "Lucas v. the South Carolina Coastal Council." The date was set for March 2nd, 1992. We had taken the next step.

I felt like I had been relieved of a ten thousand pound weight. The agents in the next room had a meal of crow to eat and I was just happy to be the one to serve it up to them. I hung up the phone and in spite of trying to keep a lid on my emotions, I broke into a huge grin.

I felt light-headed. My face felt flushed. I don't think that until that moment I had realized what a huge amount of pressure I had been under. What a relief! My job was not over, however. I still had to convince those reluctant bankers that they were dealing with a winner.

I walked back into the room and managed to quell my "I told you so" manner a little bit. I gave them the good news. No elation passed over their faces. It was almost as if they were vultures that had lost their meal. The carcass was alive and moving again. Instead of a look of satisfaction, they were forced to relent and grant the condemned man a reprieve. They were about to get rid of me and this problem loan once and for all and now I had gained new life. I am still amazed at the lack of vision this crowd showed. After more consultation, they agreed to wait for the official word and to review it with their attorney before giving me their decision.

I knew then, however, that I had gained a little more time with them before they pulled the plug and tried to back out of our agreement. Even these heartless collection agents could see that we had a chance to pay them back in full. Their greed won out when they realized that I still had a chance. They never expressed any sentiment that the outcome of this case was important to everybody who owned property, and to their occupations. A few days later they compromised and allowed me to keep some of the funds from the sale, but they still weren't interested in helping me pay the legal expenses of my case.

The next few weeks were spent getting the case ready for argument. Many hours of research were needed to become properly prepared for the full briefing of the case. Over the past few months I had begun to understand the principles of law involved. Like most Americans, I felt that private property was protected by our courts. I thought only communists and socialists were for the abolition of private property.

I was personally involved in a fight against people who wanted to destroy private property rights here in South Carolina. It was inconceivable to me that this was even an issue in my own country. This most basic freedom was denied to people in other countries and fought for all over the world, not in a U.S. Court. How had this happened to me?

Up until now, I thought this was an isolated event, confined to the peculiarities of the state of South Carolina by an overzealous, but well meaning General Assembly and its enforcement agency, the South Carolina Coastal Council. I was beginning to find out just how mistaken I had been about the sanctity of private property in this country.

The national news media began to show an interest in the case. In the press the case was portrayed as either a David versus Goliath battle or as a danger to the entire environmental movement, depending on the point of view of the writer. Requests for interviews began to come fast and furious as March 2, 1992 approached. Our case was featured in all the major magazines. I was interviewed by..... (should I mention names and conversations, I think so)....... ABC, NBC, CBS, and CNN. The C-span network did the most in-depth report. It lasted for an entire hour and gave both sides an equal hearing.

All of the things that I had heard about the way the press distorts what you say is true. Although, sometimes the distortions had to do more with the lack of airtime, than it did to biased reporting. Newspaper and magazine articles were often distorted, and I had to endure some personal hatchet jobs and unbalanced legal arguments. *Time* magazine gave me the biggest chop of the hatchet. They never addressed the issues of private property at all. They treated the entire case as a threat to the environment. The writer painted a picture that had nothing to do with the issues of the case. His article was all about hugging trees and cuddling warm and fuzzy things. People didn't count. In the middle of the article was a cartoon that looked like a blackmail letter that read: "Give me a million dollars or you'll never see the spotted owl again."

As the publicity about the case and the debate on its impact on government grew, I found that I was by no means alone. I had always thought that the environmental movement had targeted big business and major polluters, and I knew they had also tried to slow down growth through my experience as a developer at Wild Dunes. But now I discovered that the shadow of the environmental radicals and their government minions was darkening the lives of average citizens as well as corporate America. Soon after the news media started to publicize the case, I began to receive phone calls at home. At first, it was just once in a while, soon it was two or three calls a week. Letters from people as far away as Washington State and California started arriving. Each letter was about problems with regulations that had deprived them of the use of their property. The taking of property without compensation was occurring all over this country, and a lot of these folks didn't have the funds to fight back.

These Americans were from all walks of life. I heard from farmers, ranchers, disabled Vietnam vets, retirees, single working mothers, newlywed couples, homeowners, blue collar workers, and white collar yuppies. They were from every region of the United States. I got calls and letters from Minnesota, Washington, Indiana, Florida, California, Texas, and North Carolina, just to name a few.

Almost every night the telephone would ring and a tentative voice would ask if I was the David Lucas involved with the Supreme Court case. When I answered yes, they would sigh with relief and tell me that they were sorry to bother me. I would always do my best to put them at ease and usually succeeded. Reassured that they were not in any way annoying me, they would open up and tell me another heartbreaking story of the confiscation of their home and property by government.

The offending government agency would usually be different, but the story line was always the same. Some regulator had interfered in the use of their property and their lives with disastrous consequences. In many cases families were financially ruined.

In each instance, it seemed to me that these innocent people were just trying to live their lives and survive in an already difficult world, when along comes Mr. Bureaucrat and changes the rules. At first, I was alarmed to find so many of the same kind of abuses that I was having to endure. Then I became angry as the stories became more and more ridiculous. This was turning into a tidal wave that seemed about to swamp our American way of life.

As the stories began to pile up, I started to realize that this environmentally disguised attack on private property was much more widespread and more far reaching than even I had suspected. There seemed to be a concentrated movement afoot to gut the Fifth Amendment and to control private property for the good of the environment and all else be damned. I consider myself an environmentalist. But, this was just plain wrong.

It was very discouraging to know that these government agencies were getting away with this land grab in almost every instance and nobody seemed to know how to stop it. I realized that this Supreme Court case was no longer just a fight between David and Goliath, but possibly the last stand of private property in America. Our private property backs were against the wall. If we lost this battle, private property could face annihilation. If the State of South Carolina could destroy the value of my property without compensation by their unconstitutional lawmaking, then governments would have the ability to control any and all property in America. The guarantees of our beloved constitution would be turned into no more than empty promises.

After government had gained control of private property, next would come the rule of any special interest faction that could gain power. The end of freedom in this country would follow if we failed to protect the cornerstone of all liberty, private property. I agreed with John Dickinson (a Delaware delegate to the Constitutional Convention) who said long ago that liberty is best described "in the Holy Scriptures... in these expressions: when every man shall sit under his vine, and under his fig tree, and *no one shall make him afraid.*"[1] As I pondered these words, I understood the importance and the magnitude of what we were trying to accomplish. At times, I felt that there was no way to lose. This was America and my fears were unjustified. Private property had, after all, just won the Cold War. Now, the rest of the world was recognizing the value of private property.

Then I would see on television or read in the newspaper the comments of the opposition. When I heard Wayne Beam, the executive director of the South Carolina Coastal Council say on C-Span that I, as an individual, should be forced to sacrifice for the good of society, I knew that I was not overreacting. I was in a unique position to understand the consequences of what was happening all over the land. Our governments no longer respected private property. It was that plain and simple. Not only was government not protecting its citizens, it had become the oppressor.

Private Property, the bedrock of the free enterprise system, that had made America the most envied and imitated system in the history of the world, was the most endangered species of all. We had to win this fight.

As the time to prepare grew short, interested

parties filed friend-of-the-court briefs. In legalese, they are called amicus briefs. There were forty-two briefs filed on our behalf and seventy-one filed in opposition to us. The importance of the case became apparent to me when I saw the list of the enemies filing briefs against me. Many environmental groups as well as some governmental agencies concerned with losing their recently usurped powers to regulate filed opposing briefs. There is a saying that you can tell how far you have gotten by the quality of your enemies. I had come a long way.

In a quest for favorable amicus briefs, an interesting side story took place. I had been told that the Solicitor General of the United States was considered to be the tenth justice of the Supreme Court. In 1992 the Solicitor General was Kenneth Starr. The conventional wisdom was that a brief from his office carried a lot of weight with the Supreme Court Justices. So I began to call my political friends in Washington. They gave me a name and I quickly contacted that person. He was very interested and assured me that they were looking into the matter and he felt certain they would be filing an amicus brief in the case.

Days went by and I couldn't understand why the Bush Administration had shown such little interest in this issue. After all, the Vice President had often spoken in favor of property rights.

On the other hand, Bush had made that unfortunate statement about "no net loss of wetlands." Finally a brief was filed by the Solicitor General's office and it was vintage Bush Administration. It straddled the fence and was in effect, useless. They agreed with my legal position. But, they said the case should not be heard because I had not exhausted all of my administrative remedies. In other words, they wanted me to start the process all over again.

Even though they felt that I was right, they actually wanted me to go back to the state and reapply for a permit. They had not read very closely the 1990 amendment that precluded me from doing just that.

Later, I had the opportunity to meet some of the governments' attorneys who had participated in that decision. They told me that to even get the brief was difficult. The Bush Administration's lawyers were divided right down the middle on the issue and this was the best that the property rights guys could do.

Another national figure who filed an amicus brief on our behalf was law professor, Richard Epstein, of the University of Chicago. He is the author of the book, TAKINGS. It was used as a prop in the hearings to confirm Clarence Thomas as a Supreme Court Justice. I have had the pleasure of meeting Professor Epstein. His book is very pro-private property rights and anti-big government and I recommend it to all who are concerned about the erosion of property rights in this country.

The chairman of the Senate Judiciary Committee was Senator Joseph Biden of Delaware. During the confirmation hearings for Justice Thomas, Epstein's Book was held aloft by Sen. Biden. He brandished the book as if it contained all of the most hideous things ever imagined by mankind and accused Clarence Thomas of being a disciple of this foul, fiendish plot to limit government's ability to control private property. I don't remember the answer that Justice Thomas gave to Senator Biden that day. But, my memory was refreshed in June of 1992.

Preparations continued up until the last moment. The month of March was close at hand and travel preparations were being made. I learned that attendance was controlled and that we were to be given a certain amount of tickets for my personal use. My sister April wanted to go and of course, my wife, Martha.

The one other person I wanted to invite was, my old mentor, Raymon Finch. He was keenly aware of the import of the decision. We talked often and he had been most supportive. I called Raymon and invited him to Washington for the festivities. He accepted immediately and together we made travel plans.

The case was to be argued on a Monday. We decided to arrive in Washington for the weekend. So on Friday, February the 29th, Martha and I flew to National Airport, Washington, D.C. My attorneys were going to be preparing all weekend, but wanted to meet with me on Sunday afternoon to go over the last minute strategy for Monday's argument. Washington was beautiful. The weather was mild and pleasant. There was even a smattering of cherry blossoms on the trees around the Capital.

Raymon was animated, and excited about the coming event. He insisted on taking us out to dinner Friday evening. We visited the National Botanical Gardens the next morning and tried to relax a little before our day in court. On Sunday Martha, April, and I went down to meet with the lawyers.

We met in Camy's room. David Bederman was there. We had talked on the phone, but had never met in the flesh. He was a small guy with thinning black hair. I was surprised at his age. He was much younger than I had expected. We had talked often and I had pictured a man in his late forties. David was in his early thirties. The media had made it sound as if all people who were under forty were pro-environment and not concerned with private property. David was proof that not all young professors were liberal.

I could tell that he was excited by the twinkle in his eye and the enthusiasm in his voice. He was ready to rumble.

Jerry was there for our last meeting. He had just arrived in Washington and hadn't even unpacked. He also seemed eager to go. Jerry is fifty, black haired, and about five foot eight. He is articulate and likes to show off his legal knowledge by using big, obscure, legal words. After some of our meetings, I was forced to pull out my dictionary. Jerry and I had become good friends over the past few years. Because I was involved in two major lawsuits with him, we had spent an awful lot of time together.

Although Jerry grew up in the Bronx, in New York City, we shared a love of hunting and the outdoors. At the time, I was a partner in the best hunting land in the southeast. The name of the property is Two Rivers Farms. It is located in the forks of two of the major rivers in South Carolina, the Congaree, and the Wateree. We had the best duck hunting available in the state and maybe the entire southeast. The deer sometimes were so thick, that my old friend Johnny Ball used to call it South Carolina's answer to the Serengeti Plains of Africa. We had an abundance of quail, rabbits, doves and squirrels. The wild turkey hunting was fabulous and we even, from time to time, found wild Russian boar roaming the property.

Jerry and I hunted together at Two Rivers quite often. It was only a thirty minute drive from downtown Columbia, so it was very convenient for him. We treated the wildlife at Two Rivers as a renewable natural resource and worked diligently to ensure that the wildlife habitat was kept in the best shape possible. Yes, we do consider ourselves the true environmentalists. The partners in Two Rivers spent thousands of dollars and thousands of hours in those fields, swamps, rivers and ponds that made up Two Rivers Farms, proving their love for the environment.

Camy was to be the one to actually speak for me before the Supreme Court. At over six feet tall, and now over 200 pounds, Camy possesses an imposing physical presence. His manner is direct and sometimes gruff, reminding one today more of a tough inside linebacker than a slick quarterback. He is very articulate, while at the same time remaining plainspoken.

With Camy you usually didn't have to ask him to repeat or to clarify anything that he said. He had a commanding size and matched it with his intellect. His arguments were easy even for laymen to follow and he looked like he wasn't afraid of much. That was just the image that I wanted him to project. I felt good about our team's preparation thus far, but now I wanted to hear the final strategy for the opening statement.

Since Camy had argued before the Supreme Court once before, he knew what to expect in the questioning by the justices. Professor Bederman had arranged a moot court in Atlanta a few weeks before to practice the oral argument. That had been very helpful in their hearing preparations. They had compiled a list of questions that they felt would be asked and had rehearsed their answers. This was as close to the real thing as you could get.

The justices' opinions on previous property rights' cases had been researched. Some of them would be harder than others to convince, but we felt that we had at least a fighting chance with all of them.

We went over our opening statement. Camy told us he would have to state our case in no more than two or three short lines. The reason for this was simple. The justices don't waste time. This is their show and they are in control. They start to question the lawyer right away and they don't give him much time to ramble through a long opening statement. Ours was short and to the point. I asked if we could change a word or two, but I thought he had hit the nail on the head. We were ready. There was nothing else to be done to prepare for the case, so it was time to try and relax. That evening we had dinner in Alexandria with my good friends, Linda and John O'Meara.

We had a great meal and then it was off to an uneasy sleep. There was much riding on the morrows' events.

The next morning Martha, April and I took a taxi to the Supreme Court building. We met Raymon out on the street corner in front and walked around to the side entrance. A long line of people were waiting to get in to see the show. We passed through metal detectors at the entrance. Then everyone was herded by stonefaced, uniformed guards into lines that ran out of sight toward the main courtroom. We had arrived close to the time recommended, but many others had gotten there earlier. Quite a number of people had come to hear *Lucas vs. The South Carolina Coastal Council.*

The building inside was impressive. Columns, and walls of marble surrounded us and stretched out along the file of citizens. We saw several people that we knew; mainly opponents of ours who had connections with the state. Some members of the South Carolina Coastal Council nodded slight greetings. I don't know for a fact, but I'll bet a dime to a doughnut that the taxpayers of South Carolina paid for the Coastal Council members' trip to Washington. I paid for mine.

There were some property rights' supporters that recognized me and came up to wish us good luck. This was not a festive crowd. No matter who you supported, everyone felt the import of the pending arguments. All of the people in attendance were contemplative. There was a nervous anticipation in the air, regardless of which side you favored.

It took about thirty minutes, but we finally reached the inner sanctum. I'll have to admit that I was awed with the room itself. The ceiling was so high that if there had been enough moisture in the air, it could have rained. The columns were huge—it was like being surrounded by a circle of giant, marble trees. The justices' bench was made of a very dark, beautiful wood. Curved into a crescent shape, it was massive. Behind it was a huge black curtain that hung from the ceiling. The entire place had the air of the theater about it. I was praying that it wasn't going to turn out to be the theater of the absurd in this case.

There were the usual lawyers' tables in the front of the spectators' gallery, one for each side, and a roped-off group of reserved seats behind the tables. There must have been at least room for fifty people in that reserved area.

The entrance into this area was guarded by plain clothes officers with walkie talkies in their hands and plugs in their ears. I saw that my legal team had already arrived and were seated at the left hand table facing the bench. Cotton Harness and his entourage were seated at the table on the right. My immediate group found four seats together about midway to the rear in the cheap section and we took our seats. I got up and walked down to the front to speak to my lawyers and to wish them well one last time. A U.S. Marshal stopped me and asked if I was an attorney. Indignant that I could be taken as such, I replied that I was not. I was informed that no one but attorneys were allowed in the reserved seating area.

Camy spotted me and came over long enough for me to proffer my words of good luck. That accomplished, I returned to my seat between Raymon and Martha to await the entrance of the justices. Ours was not to be the first case argued. The Court only hears two cases on a particular day. The entire argument must be completed in one hour. Each side has thirty minutes to argue its case and that's it. You use twenty five minutes for your main argument and you reserve five minutes for rebuttal. It seems like a small amount of time to present such important issues, but that is the rule. I was soon to find out that twenty five minutes in the United States Supreme Court is much longer than twenty five minutes anywhere else.

The first case to be argued was one concerning bankruptcy. It had to do with the time limitations for filing claims. I don't remember many details about the case. It seems as though some government agency was trying to reopen a bankruptcy case, even though the time limits for that type of action had expired. It sounded as if property rights was not the only area in which government was getting too big.

As soon as ten o'clock rolled around, in came the Justices. I am not ashamed to say that I was awestruck. Donned in their black robes, they quickly took their seats. They didn't waste time with formalities. The plaintiff in the case opened with a statement and was quickly interrupted by one of the justices with a penetrating question. One after the other would ask his or her question and listen to the response. Then they would comment on what was said.

The lawyer for the government's case was obviously an old pro at this. He was poised and eloquent and, in my opinion, dead wrong. The other side's lawyer got up and was as nervous as a cat on a hot tin roof. The poor guy stuttered and stammered and was clearly intimidated by his surroundings. He had a good sound argument and I thought that he had the law on his side. But when pressed by a justice on a particular issue, he would back off of his argument. It took a sympathetic sounding justice to make a comment or ask another question to help him through. The two opposing lawyers had given a sharp contrast in styles. The more I listened, the better I felt about our team. At least we seemed to have prepared properly. Everything that Camy had said about the process was right on track. Later, I was to find to my pleasure that the nervous, young lawyer won that first case. It was encouraging to know that even with his lack of poise, the right side won.

Precisely one hour of time had elapsed, the first case had been argued and our long awaited moment had arrived. They called up the case of *Lucas v. the South Carolina Coastal Council.* My throat was dry, but my eyes were riveted on Camy as he strode to the podium. Practice time was up, we were about to kick off.

Camden Lewis began the argument with the planned opening statement.

"We are here because Mr. Lucas's land has been taken without just compensation being paid. The guiding principle in such a case as this seems to rest on a determination of when justice and fairness require that the economic injuries caused by a public action should be borne by the many rather than the few. Or, when has a regulation gone too far?

Our position is that when Mr. Lucas was denied all economically viable use of his land, that those basic principles demand that Mr. Lucas be paid just compensation for the taking ".

The next hour passed, and I was satisfied with my team's performance. I thought that Camy did an excellent job of listening to the legal thoughts behind the justices' questions and answering them correctly. Every question except one had been expected and rehearsed. Rather than try to recall that hour from memory, I will give you a summary of the arguments as published by the United States Law Week. Don't worry though, I intend to comment when I feel that it is important.

ARGUMENTS BEFORE THE COURT

States Land use regulation; compensation of private property owner

The Takings Clause requirement that governments compensate owners of property taken for a public use fueled oral argument before the United States Supreme Court last week. (Lucas v. South Carolina Coastal Council, No. 91-453, argued 3/2/92)

A landowner contended that a South Carolina environmental regulation barring new construction on his seaside property entitles him to compensation because it deprived him of all economically viable uses of the land. The state replied that it need not pay because its beach management law prevents serious harm to the community. The viability of a wide variety of land use restrictions may hang in the balance.

South Carolina enacted its 1977 Coastal

Zone management Act in response to the federal Coastal Zone Management Act of 1972, which encourages states to adopt coast management programs to minimize loss of life and property caused by improper development in flood-prone, storm surge, and erosion-prone areas. The South Carolina act established coastal "critical areas," including beaches and primary oceanfront sand dunes. The act directed the South Carolina Coastal Council to develop an erosion control policy, and authorized it to issue permits for development within critical areas.

Petitioner David Lucas purchased two vacant lots in a residential zone on the Isle of Palms on South Carolina's coast in 1986, with the intent of building a house on each property. The line demarcating "critical areas" was then seaward of those lots, and there were homes on adjacent lots, which cost $975,000, and are approximately 300 feet from the ocean.

In 1988, South Carolina enacted the Beachfront Management Act to provide additional protection for beaches and dunes. Under that statute, the council established a "baseline" in erosion zones at the most landward point of erosion during the past 40 years (unless data indicated that the shoreline was unlikely to return to that point). The council then drew a setback line landward of the baseline by a distance of 40 times the annual erosion rate, but no less that 20 feet. The 1988 act barred new construction seaward of the setback line, except for a "wooden walkway no larger in width that six feet."

After the council drew the new setback line landward of his lots, Lucas sued, alleging a taking of his property without just compensation in violation of the Fifth Amendment. The trial court ruled in favor of Lucas. It found that the council's action deprived him "of any reasonable economic use of the lots," rendering them "valueless."

The South Carolina Supreme Court reversed. It emphasized that Lucas, by failing to contest legislative findings in the 1988 act, conceded that South Carolina's beaches and dunes are "an extremely valuable public resource"; that new construction contributes to erosion and destruction of that resource; and that discouraging construction near beaches "is necessary to prevent a great public harm." It said Lucas rested, nevertheless, on the "solitary argument" that he was entitled to compensation because the council's regulatory action deprived him of "all economically viable use" of his property.

The South Carolina court said Lucas had

---

adopted the compensable taking view espoused by Chief Justice Rehnquist's dissent in Keystone Bituminous Coal Association v. De Benedictis, 480 U.S. 470, 55 LW 4326 (1987), a 5-4 decision. It declined to adopt that view, and instead applied the Keystone majority's multifactor test for determining whether a compensable taking has occurred. Factors to be considered under that test include (1) the economic impact of regulation; (2) its interference with investment-backed expectations; (3) the character of the government action (whether there is a physical invasion); and (4) the nature of the state's interest in the regulation.

When the state regulates to prevent a serious public harm, there is no taking☞, the South Carolina court said. It cited a line of United States Supreme Court cases dating from Mugler v. Kansas, 123 U.S. 623 (1887), involving a nuisance-like activity. It said Keystone "again approved the Mugler rule that, in some cases, no compensation is due regardless of the remaining worth of the property after regulation." It also noted Keystone's quote from Mugler: "All property in this country is held under the implied obligation that the owner's use of it shall not be injurious to the community." The beach control legislation "is necessary to prevent serious injury to the com-

☞ If you are swayed by this argument, turn to page 252 and read about the hypocritical actions taken by the state when *their* money was at risk. —D.L.

munity," the South Carolina court said, and thus the deprivation of all economically viable use of Lucas' lots did not amount to a taking.

DEFINING ECONOMICALLY VIABLE USE

A. Camden Lewis, of Columbia, S.C., arguing on behalf of the lot owner, told the Supreme Court that this case relates the question posed by Justice Holmes in Pennsylvania Coal Co. v. Mahon, 260 U.S. 393 (1922): When has a regulation gone too far? He said the court answered that question in Agins v. Tiburon, 447 U.S. 225 (1980): When the regulation denies all economically viable uses of land.

Are you saying Mr. Lucas's land was "completely worthless?" Justice Blackmun asked. "Would you give it to me?"

"Yes, if the taxes were paid on it," Lewis replied.

Lewis said Agins establishes a two-part test, under which a land use regulation may effect a taking if it does not "substantially advance legitimate state interests," or if it "denies an owner economically viable use of his land." He said he had not raised any challenge under the first prong in the courts below, but had relied solely on the second prong.

Justice Kennedy asked whether the Agins case applies when there is a nuisance.

Lewis answered that it does. The court

must look to the uses available before and after imposition of the regulation, he said.

Is land different from other property in this regard? Justice Scalia inquired. Suppose the property affected was a beer factory; would there be a recovery?

No, Lewis said. That's the Mugler case; and not all economic uses would have been denied. But real property is unique. There is a fundamental right to use it, live on it, and sell it, he said.

Chief Justice Rehnquist suggested that Lewis should adhere to the language of the Takings Clause, which entitles a landowner just compensation if his land is taken, without expounding on fundamental rights.

"Viable: is a good medical term, not a legal one, Blackmun observed. What does ??? economic viability mean?

That the property is worth zero, Lewis replied, "It has no uses, no value."

PUBLIC DANGER

Suppose you have vacant lots in a residential subdivision, Kennedy hypothesized. An earthquake fault line is discovered; building permits are denied because of the danger. Is there a taking?

No, Lewis replied, because it's a discovery that the land had no value in the first place.

But why can't the state say that as a result of studies here, this land has been found to be too dangerous to build on? Kennedy asked.

There is a factual difference here, in that there are houses all around Lucas' lots, Lewis said.

But there are instances in which all economically viable uses can be deprived and then there is no taking that you haven't distinguished, Kennedy said. Is your whole theory that if all economically viable use is deprived, that's the end of the case?

Lewis answered that the South Carolina Legislature never said anything about a ??? public harm existing here. That finding was a "quantum leap" in the state supreme court's opinion, he contended. The legislature talked about benefits of protecting tourism and public use of beaches, not about prevention of harms, he explained. He argued that the South Carolina Court's approach to this case should be avoided, because it would turn every regulatory taking case into an attack on the relevant statute to determine whether a nuisance is being regulated.

Justice Souter noted that the record indicates that at some point Lucas' land was under water.☜

Lewis confirmed that at one time there was

a "pond" on the property that has since dried up. But he contended that the whole land has been accreting for some time.

Justice Scalia observed that the state's brief says the South Carolina Supreme Court understood Lucas's argument to be very narrow: that any use of the police power that denies all economically viable use of land is a taking. Is that accurate? Scalia inquired.

We conceded a legitimate state interest in the legislation here, Lewis replied.

Then you want a per se rule, Scalia responded. The state says it's a taking sometimes, but not always, he added.

We'll take the two-part Agins test, Lewis said. It's an "or" test; you can't read out the "or," he insisted.

Scalia then asked if the state should be made to pay even if its action is to save a city.

If the land had value before and you take it away, then it's a taking, Lewis replied. But he said his "fallback" position would recognize a "public necessity" exception to the economically viable use rule. But that exception is not implicated here, he said.

RIPENESS

Interspersed throughout Lewis' argument were questions pertaining to ripeness of the case.

In 1990 South Carolina enacted amendments to the Beachfront Management Act that authorize the Coastal Council to issue a "special permit" to build or rebuild a structure seaward of the baseline in limited circumstances. Lucas has not applied for such a permit.

Lewis said that the amendment was in the legislative process while the case was being argued before the state supreme court. He said that court refused to consider the effect of the 1990 amendment after oral argument.

The South Carolina court's action "doesn't settle ripeness for us," Justice White stated.

The United States suggested in its amicus brief that the case is not ripe for this reason.

Rehnquist observed that between 1988 and 1990, there was no permit for which Lucas could have applied (it was stipulated that any permit available under the 1988 act would have been denied.)

Lewis agreed, but White noted that none of the courts below dealt with any temporary taking issue in this connection.

TWO EXTREME VIEWS

C.C. Harness III, general counsel of the state's Coastal Council, submitted two reasons for affirming: (1) construction on fragile beaches and dunes creates public harm☝; (2) Lucas' theory that any total deprivation of eco-

---

nomically viable use requires compensation is unprecedented.

What about Pennsylvania Coal v. Mahon? Rehnquist asked.

That case held that a Pennsylvania statute prohibiting mining that caused subsidence under certain structures amounted to a taking.

Harness replied that Pennsylvania Coal involved private harm with a high degree of diminution in value of the affected property.

"We have two extreme views here." Scalia said. Lucas says any regulation that deprives all economically viable use is compensable. On the other hand, the South Carolina Supreme Court says the public harm at issue needn't be great to justify a regulation that destroys economically viable uses.

Harness replied that the South Carolina court said Lucas never raised the latter issue, but relied solely on diminution in value. In addition, the legislative findings permitted the court to find great public harm, given the great threat to life and property involved☞. The case thus fits within the nuisance exception, Harness said.

What is the great threat here? Scalia wanted to know. Erosion to adjacent land over the next 50 years?

The threat is very real☞, Harness replied.

Erosion can uproot houses and cause them to crash into other structures; it can break sewer lines; it can contaminate water. In addition, he said, there is evidence in the record that the shoreline has been behind Lucas' lots 20 percent of the time♥ since 1949, and that his lots have been under water 50 percent of the time.

But Scalia countered by observing that people have built up and down Lucas's street.

Harness responded that the Beachfront Management Act was passed to address precisely that building pattern.

CABINING THE NUISANCE EXCEPTION

Justice O'Connor asked Harness if South Carolina could require removal of the adjacent homes under his theory.

No, he replied, for two reasons. First, you must look at the reasonable expectations of the property owners. Lucas' neighbors had already built under the older law.

Second, Harness said, you must look at the physical character of the land. South Carolina is trying to stop ongoing damage to the land. It is fairer to prevent new construction while permitting old habitations to exist until they are naturally eliminated, he said.♥

But what limitations are there under your view of what the Takings Clause requires?

♥ If you are swayed by this argument, turn to page 252 and read about the hypocritical actions taken by the state when *their* money was at risk. —D.L.

O'Connor asked. What line must be drawn?

If there is a great threat to public health and safety, then the state's regulatory actions are "insulated," Harness answered.☞

But suppose the danger is to the owner himself as to construction on a particular site, without regard to neighbors, O'Connor pressed.

Even then the state could prevent new construction, Harness said.

Can the state require a person living in a dangerously placed house to remove it? O'Connor asked.

Yes, without compensation, Harness said, likening that situation to tenement cases holding that the owners must remove or improve them.

Kennedy asked Harness what he thought about the Agins two-part test.

Harness said the court has never actually applied that test to require compensation. He said the test is "shorthand" indicating that courts must look at two things: diminution in value and investment-backed expectations.

Were the owner's investment-backed expectations here unreasonable as a matter of law? Kennedy asked.

Yes, Harness replied, adding that the South Carolina Supreme Court didn't have to reach

☞ If you are swayed by this argument, turn to page 252 and read about the hypocritical actions taken by the state when *their* money was at risk. —D.L.

that issue here, given Lucas' concessions regarding the legislative findings. Moreover, he noted. Lucas knew of the erosion problems on the Isle of Palms.☞

Scalia observed that the South Carolina Supreme Court drew an analogy to wetlands legislation it upheld in Carter v. South Carolina Coastal Council, 314 SE2d 327 (SC SupCt 1984), in which the court did not discuss economic viability. Wetlands legislation doesn't involve a high degree of public safety, Scalia continued. He suggested that the South Carolina court appears to say that any valid regulation of land doesn't require compensation.

That's not our position, or the South Carolina court's, Harness replied. The state court didn't have to reach that issue because it didn't have to look at harms, he said.

In any event, Harness continued, Carter rested on the principle that you can't use property in a way that harms others. No question was raised about a degree of public harm. The state's position in this case, he said, is that there is a degree of public harm that warrants insulation from application of the Takings Clause.☞

"I'm not sure where that line is," Harness conceded, observing that the court itself has dealt with the takings issue on an ad hoc basis. But that need not be decided here, given Lucas' concessions on the legislative findings, he said.

On the ripeness issue, Scalia noted that the state now argues that the case is not ripe because Lucas did not apply for a special permit under the 1990 statutory amendments. However, he pointed out that the state supreme court didn't take that position. He said the court usually goes along with the state court's position on prudential standing matters."

The above is an accurate recital of the hour long proceedings. However, it certainly can't tell you the thoughts that were running through my mind at the time. It was as if the sounds of the words had been somehow mysteriously amplified. Each question and each answer seemed to hold the issue in the balance. Even the colors and the details in the room seemed to be more vivid.

Every time that a question was asked that seemed to support our side, there was a sense of relief that this particular justice seemed to understand things the way that we did. And just as we liked some questions, others seemed to be coming from the coastal council propaganda machine.

It soon became clear, at least to me, that Justice Scalia held the same beliefs that we did and seemed disturbed with the state's case. When he started a line of questioning, we felt that the questions he posed were sympathetic to our cause. Conversely, when another Justice appeared to be weakening our position on some legal tangent, Justice Scalia would answer with either another question or a comment that would refocus the court on the real issue, which was; did the state owe me compensation for a taking under the Fifth Amendment. I loved it every time that man opened his mouth during the arguments that morning. He was knowledgeable, skillful in his questioning, and somewhat passionate in the way he articulated his understanding of the case. He was our champion that day and the champion for property rights for all Americans.

It was not as clear which way the other justices were leaning by the questions they asked or by the comments they made. Each one of the justices that spoke seemed to have a particular point of view that interested them. I realized then and there that the constitution had been deliberately written with clarity and simplicity so that everyone could read and understand it, and that it had become clouded over through the years with legal nonsense. Legal precedent had been slowly allowed to damage the purity of this remarkable document.

If we were to lose this case, the Fifth Amendment was dead and would be replaced by the rule of legislatures acting without the restraint of constitutional limitations. There would be rule by special interest factions and not by constitutional law. If you could elect your faction, then they would be able to enact legislation favorable to them and detrimental to their opposition. In other words, we would become just another banana republic so ridiculed by our society for their corruption and ineptness. I had studied this warning long ago in the Federalist Papers. Now, I was engaged in a close encounter with the very same kind of special interest factions that the Founding Fathers had worried about over two hundred years before. It was a very humbling experience to have those great men speak so directly and personally to me through the veil of time. Here I sat, a country boy from the small state of South Carolina, testing the handiwork of those distinguished men. Would the constitution prevail or be weakened by exactly what was warned against so long ago?

It seemed to me that Justice O'Connor was most vexed by the proposition that the state had a plan to force existing homeowners off of their property. She had not asked questions during Camy's argument, but had opened up on Cotton. She asked him about the states' intentions for the long term and pressed him until he admitted, reluctantly, that the state in fact did have a long term goal of forcing existing beachfront homeowners off of their land. Her line of questioning and her obvious repugnance at the specter of the state forcing citizens out of their homes seemed to put her pretty solidly in our camp.

Chief Justice Rehnquist had in previous decisions, made it clear that he was an advocate for protecting private property from unfair regulation. It was apparent in the questions he asked and in the comments he made that morning, that he felt the Fifth Amendment meant what it said. All of the other arguments were incidental to the real question.

He was also supportive of our position on the ripeness question. He stated that if the South Carolina Supreme Court had chosen to deal with the case on the merits, then there was no use in sending it back to state court for further proceedings. This is one of the most powerful weapons governments have in their vast arsenal. The courts in most cases require citizens to exhaust all of their "administrative remedies" before they can even get into court. Obviously as you are forced to deal with more layers of government, you are provided with more so-called "administrative remedies."

All this means, in most instances, is that you are forced to spend all of your money before you can even file a lawsuit. In this case, the South Carolina Supreme Court decided not to use the

slow death method of "administrative remedy."
They ruled directly on the merits of the case and
Chief Justice Rehnquist felt that the United
States Supreme Court should do the same.

Justice White seemed to disagree with Justice
Rehnquist on the ripeness issue. His limited questions and comments dealt mainly with this issue.
He even stated that the South Carolina court's action "doesn't settle the ripeness issue for us." He
worried me. I certainly was concerned by the tone
of his questions. Justice White and his prior voting
record on property rights seemed to indicate (at least
to us) that we could count on his views to be, in
general, on line with our position. The negative tone
of his ripeness questions was distressing.

The newest Justice on the court was Justice
Thomas. From every thing that we knew about
him, it seemed reasonable to conclude that he was
also a strong supporter of the Fifth Amendment.
This was particularly true considering the dialogue that had taken place during his confirmation hearings. Senator Biden was evidently
frightened by Epstein's book, and the prospect of
having the constitution enforced and governmental power curbed as intended by the framers of
our constitutional republic. It was somewhat of a
disappointment that Justice Thomas did not ask
a single question during the proceedings. With
the pain that he had endured during his confirma-

tion inquisition still very fresh and the questions by Senator Biden on the very subject now at hand, it is perhaps understandable that he took a low profile on the case.

Justice Kennedy's questioning was a little harder to read. Looking back over the *Law Week Report* on the oral arguments, it seems that he was somewhat confrontational in his approach to our position. However, when actually listening to the way his inquiries were delivered, they were done in a manner that indicated he was searching for a way to justify voting our way. In addition to my gut feeling that he was sympathetic to us, most of his writings on other property rights issues were in line with what we were asking the court to support.

Justice Souter's remarks centered on the fact that the lots had been under water at some time during the recent past. He must not have looked at the testimony from the original case. If he had, he would have realized that the beach has been building for over fifteen hundred years and was expected to continue to do so for the foreseeable future. We weren't there to argue the merits of the Beachfront Management Act. We never got notice from the legislature of what they were doing. I was never given the opportunity to testify on the need for this legislation before the bill was passed. Justice Souters' remarks seemed to follow the lead of the environmentalist's propaganda. He never asked a question that went to the heart of the constitutional issues of the case. He seemed to me to be more interested in legal technicalities and avoided the central issue which was: did the state owe me and others like me, compensation for destroying the value of property? That was a personal disappointment for me, because I had supported his nomination when it was made by President Bush. He seemed to be a puzzle, wrapped in an enigma, staring at a mirror. Winston, where are you? What is Souter's philosophy of government? I now suspect that he is much more moderate than anticipated by the American public. Or does he think that the government can do what it wants to do, if the cause is just?

Justice Blackmun asked the only question that my lawyers had not rehearsed. He asked if I would be willing to give him the two lots since we felt they had no value. This was a loaded question. Camy answered him correctly. He said that we would give him the lots if he would be willing to pay the taxes on the property. Of course, it really depended on the way the Supreme Court ruled. If they ruled in our favor, then the lots would only have salvage value determined by a court. At this point in our legal odessey, the two lots were not an asset for me. In fact, they were a real financial liability. I still was required to pay the property taxes due each year. In addition, I was liable as the owner of the property for any accidents that happened on them, so I had to carry insurance—which sure wasn't free.

Blackmun asked a couple of questions dealing with the definition of economically viable value. From his comments he appeared to be leaning towards the position that just because the lots exist, they have to have value. This is a good academic exercise, but not worth much in the real world. This line of thought was so far from reality that I discounted it as a serious threat to our position. In the world of modern American jurisprudence, however, my way of thinking is out of line with a lot of judges.

I don't have a visual recollection of Justice Stevens. Nor do I remember if he asked anything at the hearing. Both of these senses: sight and hearing, are acutely attuned when you are in the situation that I was in that day. Of all the nine Justices, I have no recollection of that man at all. Each of the others I can still picture in my mind's eye. I remember their expressions. I was even paying attention to their body language and the tone of voice of all of the other eight members. But, I do not remember Justice Stevens.

We had taken twenty-five minutes of our allotted thirty in our opening argument. We had five minutes left in which to add to our statements or to rebut something the state had brought up in it's argument. Chief Justice Rehnquist asked if we had anything more to add. I looked at Raymon and we both said under our breath that we hoped not. I felt good about what had taken place. We had responded well and had kept our arguments focused. It was time to stop talking.

Cotton Harness had the worst of it that morning, in my opinion. When he answered that the state had the right to force people out of their homes without compensation, I think that was the clear turning point, if there was one that morning. If the state was allowed to create, by legislation, a new nuisance whenever it wanted to, then constitutional government was dead in the United States and we would have rule by majority. Legislative tyranny can be just as bad as the tyranny of a king or a dictator. Cotton's argument of protecting people from themselves didn't carry much personal conviction or power. His had not been a very compelling debate, and I sensed that most of the justices agreed. But unfortunately, I didn't have a vote.

Lawyer Harness had even tried to use the remaining value argument. With a straight face, he said that I could enjoy my lot by building an observation deck on it. I could exclude others from the property. From time to time, I could even pitch a tent on the lots. In short, I could enjoy the most expensive camping and picnic site in the world. That was, he contended, enough value to allow the state to escape paying for the lots. Of course, the deed restrictions in place at Wild Dunes would have prevented me from either pitching a tent or from building open camp fires on the lots. So, I would be denied even the limited uses proffered by my opponents. This was a preposterous argument even if I could have camped or built fires on those lots. I could have gone to one of South Carolina's ocean-front state parks for a hell of a lot less money than I had shelled out for those two lots. Unfortunately, this kind of foolish argument is sometimes taken seriously by a court when argued with conviction by almost all of the environmental groups in the country. Justice Scalia's observation on that subject is worth mentioning here. He said something to the effect that for a million dollar investment, Mr. Lucas had more in mind than playing in the sand.

Camy, Jerry, and David put their heads together. Camy then stood and said to the court " We have nothing further to add, but we will be glad to answer any other questions."

Justice Rehnquist looked around at the other Justices. Most were already leaning forward in their chairs; their body language telling him they were through. Hearing no other questions, he rose and court was dismissed. My fate, and the fate of the Fifth Amendment was now in the hands of eight men and one woman.

I turned to Raymon and he said to me, "For God so loved the world that he didn't send a committee." I still prayed that this committee was sent by God to help me and save the Fifth Amendment.

8
WHO ME, MAKE SPEECHES?

OR:

WILL HE EVER SHUT UP?

After the Justices disappeared behind that huge black curtain, everyone stood up and headed for the exits. Raymon, Martha, April and I went up to congratulate our attorneys. With one or two exceptions, we all agreed that the arguments had gone well. We discussed the case with the lawyers as we walked out to find some lunch. I was famished and very thirsty. Watching your future being decided was hard work. My lawyers were definitely ready for some refreshment after their presentation. Although they felt very good about the way it had gone, from their legal experience, they cautioned me against reading too much into the questions that had been asked by the Justices.

That was the advice they gave to me, but as soon as it left their mouths, they began to go through the same analysis. Some lawyers are, after all, human (don't worry, I know my share of lawyer jokes). As we walked together towards those huge doors leading to the sunshine, many of the other spectators joined in on our little traveling conversation. Most of them agreed that our arguments had gone well, and that the justices seemed supportive of our position.

Several people introduced themselves as supporters of our cause and were optimistic. All of them commented that Justice Scalia had been very effective in making the case for us. Even a few of the members of the South Carolina Coastal Council, had become noticeably more friendly towards our party. Maybe this was a sign of things to come. I sure hoped so.

As we made our way through the door, I was approached by a neatly dressed man who, with great enthusiasm, thanked me for fighting my way to the Supreme Court. He introduced himself as Roger Pelon of the Cato Institute. I had long been an admirer of the Cato Institute and had recently read an article that had been pro-Lucas in the *Wall Street Journal*. Roger had written the piece, and I wanted to spend some time talking with him, but the news media had set up the cameras and microphones at the bottom of the steps.

Roger walked with me down those long granite steps toward the cameras. He was offering encouragement with each step we took. A few more well wishers that hadn't been able to get inside to hear the arguments came up and introduced themselves. They too, thanked us for our efforts and wished us good luck. It was too late for that now. It was in other hands. "Go get 'em," Roger said, as he moved off into the crowd and I turned to face the press.

As I reached the bottom of those long granite steps, someone directed me towards the bank of microphones and cameras. I had done quite a few interviews before, but they were with a seemingly neutral press. Waiting was a whole gaggle of the nation's press corp, and I was expecting a much more hostile atmosphere here in Washington, than back home in South Carolina. I was not to be disappointed.

The questions came fast and furious like verbal hand grenades. I think there was some fear among members of the Washington press corps, that this case could mean a sweeping curtailment of governments' powers to regulate. If I won, and the state was required to pay compensation, then budget considerations would naturally limit their ability to take other people's property. It was definitely what I was hoping for and that was one of the main reasons that I had pressed the case. The special interest groups who had been successful in using big government to pass their special agendas were fearful of the same thing. Most of the press that day seemed to be sympathetic to the environmental special interest groups and big government agendas, and not to private property owners.

We finally finished the interviews and went to lunch. All of my attorneys and their wives came. Raymon also joined us. The discussion, of course, centered on the exchange of impressions. We felt confident that we would prevail after analyzing what the justices had said. Each of us predicted the vote count. The lowest score anticipated was a five to four win for us. Hopelessly optimistic, I foresaw a nine to zip win. Of course, I still think General Lee can win at Gettysburg every time I read about that battle in the history books. Armed with this bolstered attitude of an imminent victory, we all caught flights home to await the opinion of the nine people who really mattered.

There was much publicity generated during the next few months. Editorials both favorable and unfavorable were sent to me by people from all over the country. One reporter, after the press conference on the steps of the Supreme Court, had told me there was more press in attendance than he had seen for any other case in the past twenty years. All of this exposure generated more and more telephone calls. People from all over America began to call and ask to speak to the David Lucas who was fighting the state of South Carolina. This became quite a joke, because there are five David Lucas's in the Charleston area and I am the third one listed in the telephone book. So each caller had generally talked to two other households before they found the right one. All of the people were very kind, and I was happy to talk with them. Soon, it was a nightly occurrence. The phone would ring and I would listen to another story of a government taking of property.

Letters of support and encouragement also began to arrive. Just a few at first, but more and more began to pour in as time passed. The taking of property was happening all over the country. People were losing their land to all levels of government. It was not only the environmentalists that were, in effect, behind the government's confiscation of property. If the environmental regulators could get away without paying compensation, then why should any governmental agency have to pay. The cancer of regulatory theft was widespread in the country and growing at a tremendous pace. *Lucas v. The South Carolina Coastal Council* was being looked upon as the case that would either stop the spread of this cancer and send it into remission, or allow "regulationitis" to spread throughout the body politic and kill the patient.

I had believed for a long time that governments at all levels were growing too large and powerful, but it was much worse than even I had imagined. I had expected a few isolated cases like mine to come to light. But the trickle that I had expected had turned into a flood. There was something terribly wrong happening to ordinary people all over this country.

At first, I had gotten calls from small real estate developers. They were being destroyed financially. I had assumed that established business interest groups had been fighting to stop this sort of thing. After all, they had the money, manpower, influence, and the interest at risk to fight this menace. It had seemed logical that big business would have been leading the charge, so I began to look around to see which big corporations were supporting property rights. I had read that big business was behind such entities as the 'wise use' movement out west, and were leaders in the property rights fight. So, I thought that at some point they would be contacting me. But, as the number of calls increased, the proportion of developers declined. More and more, the calls were from individuals and small business owners who had my kind of problem, but who were not in a position to defend their land or if they had tried, had either run out of money, or hit a stone wall with some government bureaucracy or court. Big business was not showing up in any of the constant stream of property rights stories.

Each one of these new friends of mine was desperate and mystified as to why this was happening in the land of the free. I had calls from retired World War II veterans who had bought property for their retirement only to find out that their land had suddenly become wetlands. This made their land useless and therefore, totally worthless. One distraught D Day veteran said that he had risked his life in service to his government, and it had taken his land. He wondered what he had fought for.

One Vietnam veteran told a story of losing his land because of the Army Corp of Engineers. It seems that his mother and he owned a parcel of land in coastal North Carolina. They intended to develop it for the residential use for which it was zoned. They needed to build a causeway across an old mill pond area for access to the prime property. Permits for the road were given and the road was built. Before it could be finished, however, some group objected and threatened suit. The Corp of Engineers caved in to this special interest group and reversed itself.

They ordered the almost finished causeway to be torn out. When this veteran refused to do so, the Corp threatened to put him in jail. When this didn't work, they threatened to put his mother in jail. When even this dastardly tactic failed to get the intended response, they threatened the contractor who had built the road with fines and jail time.

The contractor lost his nerve and went in and tore out the road that he had just constructed. Then, to add insult to injury, the contractor sued the vet and his mother for reimbursement for the cost of destroying their property. I was astounded by this. But the real heartbreak occurred in the next paragraph of his letter. He thanked me for carrying on the fight and said that he was a wheelchair bound disabled Vietnam Veteran who had given his future to his country. And now his country had taken away his only asset. It had ruined both this man and his mother financially. When I finished his letter, I felt that I had been reading a story that could only have taken place in another country. The only difference was that they didn't put him in a camp up on the northern slopes of the Alaskan tundra.

I was depressed and touched by this story, in particular. But it didn't stay number one for long. Other stories, just as unbelievable continued to come to my attention. A divorced mother, trying to support her two teenage children, had earned a decent living for her family by building a few houses each year to supplement her income as a real estate saleswoman. Then she ran afoul of some county zoning ordinance that had to do with water run off. They refused to give her an occupancy permit because of the way one inspector decided to interpreted this new regulation.

After trying unsuccessfully to comply with the new rules, she ran out of money and time and had lost her property through foreclosure. By the time she called me, she was dependent on her oldest daughter for food and shelter. This woman was desperate, broke, and angry. Unfortunately, she was not alone.

It wasn't long before I had gotten calls from almost every state in the union. Something was definitely wrong in this country. I was discovering that my case was just the tip of the iceberg. And the fact was, it was a huge iceberg and growing at a phenomenal rate every day.

Invitations to tell my story to different groups began to come in on a regular basis. A lot of people had seen the press conferences and the interviews and I guess they liked what I had to say. I had only given a few speeches previously and that was to small groups of people that I knew. That was about to change. Evidently, my real life David-versus-Goliath story really offered hope to people who were feeling the powerful hand of unleashed governments all over the land.

I thought that the publicity and the interest in the case would soon die down, but the number of calls grew and the offers to tell my story to the public became more numerous. No group of people had protection from this tidal wave of assault on private property. Everybody whom I talked to had one thing in common: they were all hoping that I would win the case.

9
Back To See More Judges

OR:

Hey Martha, I Think They've Redecorated the Place

Time passed slowly for us that spring. The end of June 1992 was fast approaching and we had heard nothing. The ruling had to come out by the last day of that court session and that day was June twenty-ninth. I called Jerry frequently and got about the same response, "No David, I haven't heard anything, but I assure you that as soon as I do, you'll be the first person that I call."

The decision came on the last day, June 29, 1992. It was a Monday and the verdict arrived at about ten o'clock in the morning. I received a phone call from an excited friend, Linda O'Meara, who was living in Washington, D.C. Linda had arranged to have some people standing by at the

Supreme Court, and they had just gotten a copy of the decision. I asked her if we had won and she said, "I think so, but the decision is over fifty pages long and I haven't even tried to read it." I asked Linda to turn to the last page and read the last line.

Linda said that the decision was signed by Justice Scalia. I thought to myself, "That is a very good sign." Then she said three beautiful sounding words "Reversed and Remanded." Three simple words that were music to my ears. I knew enough by now about the law to understand that we had at least won something. Linda said that she would begin faxing the decision immediately.

My fax rang and the sheets began to flow down the telephone wires from Washington to my office in Mount Pleasant. As it turned out, there were seventy two pages in Justice Scalia's majority opinion. I called Jerry to tell him the news. He was just getting his copy also by facsimile, and he told me that he would call me back as soon as he understood the ruling. He did tell me that it seemed to be a six to three opinion. We had won something with one vote to spare.

Before I could finish reading my copy, the phone started to ring. It was the press. The reporters were asking for interviews and comments. I told them that I would have to call them back after I had read the opinion. I was almost too excited to focus my eyes on the pages. Justice Scalia had prevailed. He and the majority of the Justices had ruled that the State of South Carolina had no more power to stop me from building on my land than my next door neighbor did. My neighbor had the right to stop me from doing anything on my property that was considered a common law nuisance, and the state had the same right as my neighbor. However, it did not have more of a right than my neighbor, even though the South Carolina legislature had tried to give itself more power through the 1988 Beach Front Management Act. The Supreme Court ruled that the state could not avoid compensating me by simply passing a new law and declaring a previously lawful act a nuisance.

The majority had ruled that the state had to prove that my building a house on the beach was a nuisance under the existing nuisance laws of the state to avoid paying compensation. If they could not prove that the building of a house was a common law nuisance, then the state would owe me just compensation. This was exactly what the Fifth Amendment said. In the court's opinion, the state would have a difficult time proving that building a house on my lots was a nuisance, since there were houses all around my lots and the state did not consider them a nuisance. I felt elated and vindicated.

This was the heart of the ruling. It disagreed with the police power's argument that the state had made. The state had argued that any legitimate use of the state police powers exempted them from having to compensate the owner. The United States Supreme Court said, No. Only if the police power was stopping a common law nuisance already in common acceptance, would it exempt the state from payment.

As to valuation, (how much money the state owed me), the court also ruled that when a regulation takes all economic value, that constitutes a unique category of taking, and requires compensation from the regulating body without meeting any other tests. This was good for me, but this language was to be used by property rights opponents to cloud the ruling for others. They soon began to interpret this part of the ruling as requiring a one hundred per cent devaluation before compensation is required. Justice Scalia tried to warn government regulators to beware of thinking that all economic value must be gone before the court would consider that reduction in value as a taking. In footnote number eight he said :

"Justice Stevens criticizes the 'deprivation of all economically beneficial use' rule as 'wholly arbitrary,' in that '[the] landowner whose property is diminished in value 95% recovers nothing,' while the landowner who suffers a complete elimination of value 'recovers the land's full value.' Post at ———, 120 L Ed 2d, at 844. This analysis errs in its assumption that the landowner whose deprivation is one step short of complete is not entitled to compensation. Such an owner might not be able to claim the benefit of our categorical formulation, but, as we have acknowledged time and again, '[t]he economic impact of the regulation on the claimant and ...the extent to which the regulation has interfered with distinct investment-backed expectations' are keenly relevant to takings analysis generally.

Penn Central Transportation Co v New York City, 438 US 104,124,57 L Ed 2d 631, 98 S Ct 2646 (1978). It is true that in at least some cases the landowner with 95% loss will get nothing, while the landowner with total loss will recover in full; but that occasional result is no more strange than the gross disparity between the landowner, whose premises are taken for a highway (who recovers in full), and the landowner whose property is reduced to 5% of its former value by the highway (who recovers nothing). Takings law is full of these 'all-or-nothing' situations."

This was good news. I was happy with the opinion. We had been hoping for a plain reinstatement of the lower court ruling, money damages and all. That would have ended the matter and made the law and the constitution very clear. But that was not the way it was going to be. There were definitely going to be more courts, and more lawyers, and more legal fees involved, in this most interesting time in my life (there is an old Arabian curse that says, "May your life be long *and* interesting.") Still, a victory is sweet and this was a victory on all the legal and constitutional points we had argued.

My enthusiasm was tempered somewhat when I got around to reading the dissenting opinion of Justice Blackmun. His opening sentence was, "Today the court has launched a missile to kill a mouse." Well, maybe from his point of view, but this mouse was bringing in the modern version of the economic bubonic plague and deserved to be destroyed by any means possible.

As it has turned out, this mouse refuses to admit that it is dead. After reading Justice Blackmun's writing, I could only shake my head and wonder at what lengths some people go to, to twist and torture simple reason. Instead of getting angry, I felt sorry for this man. How could someone, so dedicated to other civil rights, not recognize that the Fifth Amendment allows people to acquire property, and therefore, also acquire relative independence from economic coercion, and that this is the underpinning for all other civil rights. Of course, if I had lost the case, I would have certainly had different emotions and pity would not have been one of them.

There was much more in those seventy-two pages than I have room to give you here. For those who want the entire opinion, it is included in the back of this book. In my view, the court had done an excellent job in settling the question, "Can a regulation result in a compensable taking?" Or, in layman's terms, if a law or regulation results in a loss of value, does the regulating agency owe you money just the same as if they physically take your land for a road? The court had answered; yes. This was the heart of the ruling in my case. Regulatory takings had now been brought firmly under the umbrella protection of the Fifth Amendment of the United States Constitution.

Jerry called and agreed that we had won on all of the issues that had been argued before the court. The only question still remaining was a really big one. How much money did the state owe me? The United States Supreme Court had not yet ordered the state to write me a check. All of the hype and the excitement was still not putting any bread on my family's table. What was the next step? What, besides the legal points, had we really won? Jerry's reply was that we had won the right to go back to the South Carolina Supreme Court. How long before that took place? I was certain that we were within weeks of ending this legal odyssey. Boy, was I wrong.

We now had to prepare for an entirely new trial. Everything that was necessary to prepare for the United States Supreme Court was going to be needed again to prepare for this next hearing, the fourth one. It was the same old song with a slightly different beat. We now had the advantage of a decision by the Supreme Court of the United States of America on our side. This should put an end to this ordeal in short order, or so I thought. I had underestimated the Byzantine labyrinth of the American judicial system.

Briefs were prepared by both sides. These were needed to tell the South Carolina Supreme Court what the United States Supreme Court had said. There was only one opinion. It was written in English by Justice Scalia. It was, I grant you, legalese English, but it was still the same English spoken by both sets of attorneys. After I had read our brief on what the United States Supreme Court had said, I was given the state's brief to digest.

Their brief was an amazing attempt by the states' attorneys to rewrite the United States Supreme Court's decision. It was as if they had read something entirely different. What a racket America's lawyers have going. They get paid to disagree on things like two plus two make four. Our legal system is dominated by lawyers with degrees such as Master of Bovine Scatology. As proof, all one has to do is read those two briefs describing the same decision.

Oral arguments were scheduled to be heard in the fall. We had been given thirty days to file our petition to the South Carolina Supreme Court. The state then had thirty days to answer our brief. That meant that we would get to court at the earliest, in September of 1992. The actual date was set for late November. The wheels of justice certainly do turn slowly. I was beginning to wonder if my squeaky wheel was ever going to be greased. Actually the squeak was becoming a groan. At least things were finally moving in the right direction. The only problem was that in September I moved to Krakow, Poland.

I had been working since 1989 on a project to build low cost housing in Eastern Europe. The project seemed to be coming together and my business partners were ready to get things moving. So I went to Poland and rented an apartment. As a developer of real estate, it was interesting to see what happens to a society that does not protect private property. My sojourn in Poland reinforced my belief that the right to private property is the basis of all other personal liberties. Ask those who have been there. I think that you will find that ninety-nine percent of them will agree with me. A society that does not protect the rights to own and use private property is a hopeless society. It was strong irony that I, of all people, would be living and working in a formerly communist country that was just trying to recover their lost property rights. Truth is sometimes stranger than fiction.

There is a six hour time difference between South Carolina and Poland. So, while I was at work in Poland, my attorneys were asleep. When they got to the office they would fax me material for review. I was able to read and make comments on it almost immediately.

We decided that it would not be necessary for me to be there in person for our return to the South Carolina Supreme Court. Any comment that I made to the press could adversely affect my case, so I decided to remain in Poland. It was not easy waiting.

One of my business associates was a Polish national hero. He had been a leader in the Solidarity Movement in the Krakow region of Southern Poland. His name was Leslaw Kuzai. Leslaw had been active in organizing demonstrations against the communist Polish government. He had been caught by the secret police and had spent two years in the police dungeons. I won't go into detail here, but it was not pleasant. I had long conversations with him and he was shocked to find out that a case like mine could even come up in America. One day he said something that I shall never forget.

"David, it can be done. We beat the communists in their own backyard. I am sure that you can defeat them in America."

Leslaw and almost all of the Eastern Europeans that I met spoke the word *America* with a kind of reverence. It was difficult for me to have to explain to them that the America of their dreams was quickly becoming the nightmare of their past! I was living proof that it was happening. This time, not in the name of the workers of the world, but in the name of the world itself.

From what I have seen of the job Poland did for the workers of the world, I don't think that we want or need the same kind of results for mother Earth.

One of our projects was in a small suburb of Krakow. I had to present the development plans to the city council. There were forty council members and the plan was to be discussed and put to a vote. None of the town officials or council members spoke English. I would have to use a translator to explain the project to them. From my experience with these kinds of presentations to similar city councils back home, I assumed this was going to be difficult. Krakow is one of the most polluted environments in Eastern Europe. I fully expected a full blown Greenpeace demonstration outside the council chamber. At the very least I was expecting some tough questions that would be doubly difficult to handle because of the language barrier.

The meeting began and I presented my plan to the council. I showed them the layout of the lots, then passed around the various house plans that we proposed building. After everyone had a chance to go over the information it was time for the questions. Just as I had expected, there were lots of questions by the council members, but not the kind I expected.

"How soon can you get started?" was the first question.

"Will they be affordable?"

"Is your kind of building going to be of wood or stone?" was asked.

"Can anyone buy these houses or will you have to get on a list?" was one with a lot of meaning, coming from those who had lived under communism.

"When these are sold, will you stay here and build more?"

These people were desperate for housing. Under communism, the waiting period for government housing was over ten years. The homes were all the same; usually small, 500 square foot apartments in an eleven story high-rise with only a small elevator. They wanted good, inexpensive housing as quickly as possible. There were ten thousand families on the list in this village alone. In Poland itself, they needed over three million units, immediately. Our development plan passed unanimously.

After the meeting ended, the mayor and city officials came up to me and apologized for asking so many questions. They were sorry for the shabby way that the council had treated me and begged my forgiveness. The Mayor said through the interpreter that he was sure that I was not used to this kind of treatment in America. He assured me that the Poles would learn from America and the next time things would go better. I did not have the heart to explain to him that the America that he thought he knew, now existed only in history books. That was a poignant day in my life.

As it turned out my presence was not needed back in the South Carolina Supreme Court. My wife, Martha stood in for me with the press, and did a wonderful job. Martha handled the press like a professional. She called me as soon as the arguments were finished and said that our attorneys were well prepared and had performed well. Camy and Jerry once again put forth a great argument.

Martha told me that the states attorney, our old friend Cotton Harness, attempted to retry the entire case. He tried to bring up issues that had not even been before either the state or federal Supreme Courts in either of the previous two arguments. To their credit, the South Carolina Supreme Court would not hear it.

Justice Toal, to everyone's surprise, took the lead in shutting off this attempt by the state to retry the entire case. You may recall that it was Toal who had authored the South Carolina Supreme Court's original decision against me. This time, she firmly instructed Mr. Harness to return to the issue at hand. She said, "We are not here to retry the case, only to try to interpret the ruling of the high court and apply it appropriately to South Carolina law." Will wonders never cease?

The only question before the court was; could the state of South Carolina prove that building a house on my two lots constitute a common law nuisance under the laws of South Carolina? If they could, which was most unlikely, then they didn't owe me "just compensation." If they could not, they would have to pay for a taking.

Harness attempted to prove that it was a nuisance but, Martha felt, without any success. It was now time to wait. The last time we waited on a decision from the South Carolina Supreme Court it took a year. The Bible says that a day to the Lord is a thousand years. I know exactly how God feels.

Mercifully, this time things were different. The Court issued its order within three weeks. I was astounded that they reached a decision so quickly. I fully expected it to take at least another six months or more. The order was another win for us. The Court ruled that there was no common law nuisance violation involved in building houses on my two lots. Therefore, a compensable taking had occurred. Eureka, they finally found it!

They held, that since the state had amended the 1988 law to allow construction under special building permits, the taking was temporary. What was this? The Court ruled that the temporary taking had occurred from the date that the law was passed in 1988 until the date of the court's ruling in November of 1992. That meant that the state of South Carolina owed me compensation for four years. But what did they owe me? The court ruled that we would have to go back to lower court for a fifth trial.

The fifth trial would determine finally, how much money was owed. After all, that was really what the case was all about. Who pays for these laws, the society that derives some supposed benefits or the individual who derives ruin and no benefits. The South Carolina Supreme Court then cited two cases that would control what damages I would be allowed to recover. This was just what I wanted for Christmas: no money and another trial.

The court also cautioned the state that if I applied for a permit at some time in the future, and the permit was not granted, or if it was granted with restrictions, then I was not precluded from bringing another lawsuit to clear up that point. What was this? The court was inviting me to sue on new grounds. This would be a brand new lawsuit and I could start the process all over again. How thoughtful of them to allow the games to continue.

This court system is an amazing money making scheme for the legal profession. It's a very simple, and predictable system. All the courts have to do is never give a clear or complete decision. They must not settle problems in a way that would allow the victim (client) to escape the trap. This way, there is always room for more lucrative litigation. I think this is the reason so many lawyers wear gray suits. It continually reminds judges to keep things in gray areas. Never say something is black or white. All decisions must be rendered in only shades of gray. So on it goes, year after year, month after month, day after day, and most importantly, dollar after dollar.

After four years and hundreds of thousands of dollars in legal fees, I had won the right to waste more time, pay more legal fees, and run the risk of not winning any money.

By this time I knew the legal drill well. We had to prepare once again for trial, as if it were a brand new case. In every court but one, we had won all the legal arguments, but no money. Now, we were forced to go back into the court system once again. There would be more depositions taken, more briefs written and submitted, more arguments made to the court, more rulings issued, and then another appeal to see just how much time, money and life can be squeezed out of the idiot (client) trapped in this Alice-In-Wonderland judicial system. Now I know why the Cheshire Cat had such a big grin. He was a lawyer.

I didn't understand why the court didn't just reinstate the lower court's ruling and pay the interest due for the time of the taking. That would be too simple and for goodness sakes what would the lawyers and the courts do with all that free time on their hands? But, enough lawyer bashing, for now. My sister, who is an attorney, won't let me go on.

There was nothing to do but keep dancing with the nine hundred pound gorilla. I was getting pretty tired of the fast polka but I sure couldn't let go now. If the gorilla stepped on me, well, I could stand sore feet, but I didn't relish the thought of fallen arches. I returned from Poland and we started to prepare for the next dance.

The state decided to hire an outside attorney to replace our old legal antagonist, Cotton Harness. They chose a local Charleston firm. I had known this new lawyer for a long time socially. His name was Backmon Smith. He was the third or the fifth or the seventh Backmon Smith, I can't remember which. This is important to note, because lawyers get to charge more if they have those numbers behind their names. I think that it has a multiplier effect on their billings.

The South Carolina Coastal Council was determined to do everything in its power to frustrate the courts, the U.S. Constitution, the South Carolina Constitution, justice, fairness, common sense, and its own citizen, David Henry Lucas. Cost to the taxpayers of South Carolina was, of course, no object.

Once again, we had thirty days to state our case in a written brief. Then the state had thirty days to react with their brief. When we got Backmon's brief it seemed as if he had not read any of the material from the first four trials. I was assured that it was "only a legal tactic designed to frustrate." It worked. I was really frustrated.

After all of this, we still had to supplement what we had said in relation to what they had answered. They, of course, had time to react to our reaction. Next, it was time to take and give depositions. This would be a great Bud Abbot and Lou Costello routine. I felt like Costello doing the Whose-On-First bit. The only problem is that Costello's routine only took ten minutes, and my act was turning into The Never Ending Story.

If no one else needed any extra time, then the court would set a trial date. Of course, the date would be set after consulting with each lawyer to make sure that his schedule was not in conflict with something else that he might have to do that was more important. Things such as attend a very prestigious legal conference somewhere near Miami, or play in the South Carolina Bar Association's annual golf tournament at Seapines Plantation on Hilton Head Island or go on a vacation that, of course, had been planned for over six months.

Delays are a way of life in our legal system. In the meantime, I am dying the slow death of financial strangulation. But never mind, that's the way the American court system works or doesn't work depending on your point of view. If you are the plaintiff, trying to recover damages, delays are agonizing. If, however, you are a defendant that might have to write a check some day, then delays are your best friend. Go figure.

The South Carolina Supreme Court's order on Remand directed "the parties to amend their pleadings and present evidence of the actual damages Lucas has sustained as a result of the State's temporary nonacquisitory taking of his property without just compensation." At the court's direction, Jerry and Camy filed an amended complaint. Paragraph twelve of that complaint contained an allegation that I was entitled to a building permit. This was a simple allegation considering that the court's order also stated that the "Coastal Council could deny the special permit or place such restrictions on the permit that Lucas might contend a subsequent unconstitutional taking has occurred." Incredibly, the reply from the Coastal Council was "DENIED." I wasn't shocked or surprised. I was delighted. Let me tell you why.

Property owners had requested and received building permits on some of the other lots that had been affected by the Beachfront Management Act. They had been issued permits under the 1990 Amendment to the 1988 Beachfront Management Act. This was discrimination. They had violated my civil rights by granting other lot owners a building permit, but denying me the same. That was against the law. As a matter of fact, it violated section 1983 of the Civil Rights Act. I was getting pretty good at providing interesting dilemmas for my lawyers. I didn't want to see them lose their interest in this five year old case. The obvious solution was for them to file an action under the Civil Rights Act. They were glad to oblige. Just imagine, an entirely new lawsuit. Perhaps this one would take five more years and then we could find an entirely new cause of action and begin the process again.

This new lawsuit wasn't nearly as much fun for the members of the South Carolina Coastal Council. Under this action, they were sued personally. It was no longer just my money and the taxpayer's money at risk. Now, those sanctimonious ladies and gentlemen could no longer afford to just play disinterested party. They were now at risk personally. Their money and their assets were on the line. Now they would feel the stress of litigation along with me, up close and personal. They would have to go out and hire a lawyer. What would they do now?

The answer came the next day. They held an "emergency meeting" behind closed doors. We were contacted immediately by Mr. Smith, Esquire. He proposed that we enter into "serious" settlement negotiations. This had gone on long enough, it seemed. So, in the best interest of all concerned parties, it would be better to settle the case. It's amazing how much wisdom can be suddenly acquired when your bank account is on the line. I wonder how they would have acted had they been on the hook for five years instead of just a few days?

Settlement negotiations began to take place. We had determined that my damages were around three million dollars. The risk to our case going to trial was that a jury would realize that any award would come from the state's coffers and that they as taxpayers, would be partially paying the money awarded to me. This was not good. If we had been suing a major corporation, then a jury would be prone to act differently. With this in mind, we began to trade offers with the state.

When the state offered one million five hundred seventy-five thousand dollars for the purchase of the lots, things got serious. The negotiations with the state were pretty tough. But they did not rival the negotiations with the bank and its collection agency. They didn't want me to go to trial and risk losing it all, and yet they didn't want me to have any money either. I love negotiating with those bank guys almost as much as I like being poked in the eye with a sharp stick.

We finally reached an agreement with all parties concerned and settled the case in July of 1993. The state took title to the lots. In return I received one million five hundred seventy five thousand dollars. I then immediately paid the bank nine hundred thousand dollars, and my attorneys took five hundred and fourteen thousand dollars in fees. Then I had to pay all of the expenses of my legal team, and that amounted to several thousand dollars more. After paying several other back debts that had accumulated over the past five years, I was left with less than ten thousand dollars out of that one million five hundred seventy-five thousand dollar sales price.

This didn't seem fair. It wasn't going to be the "just compensation" that the constitution said I should receive. My damages had been close to three million dollars and so I lost over one and a half million; but I really had no choice. It was time to let discretion become the better part of valor. I was dangerously low on capital (broke in layman's terms) and I faced an uncertain result with a jury trial as I outlined above. The bank was pressuring me to accept the settlement. Things were getting tight. So, I decided to settle the case.

From a philosophical point of view, some good things happened. The Coastal Council was forced to pay for part of the settlement from its budget. The rest was made up from the general coffers of the state. This was personally, a financial Pyrrhic victory. But there were some sharp teeth in this bite for the bureaucrats. A lot of money was paid out and that had to hurt the other side. At least, I don't think the Coastal Council staff got any raises that year. The legal point had been won. A sizable compensation award had actually been paid in a regulatory takings case. It had been worth the fight for me to accomplish this.

The only thing left to collect was the twenty thousand dollars in property taxes I had paid during the time my property had been rendered useless. I had asked the county to return my money, but as usual they said, "so sue me." I did. I'm still fighting that little battle. Nothing is simple these days. I once was critical of people who were always involved in litigation. My, my, how times have changed.

Shortly after the case was settled, the state budget and control board met. They decided that instead of keeping the lots for the glory of nature and posterity, they would sell them to the highest bidder and issue that person a building permit.

They issued a statement that even I couldn't believe. They said, in part, that since there are houses on either side of the lots and houses all around, it doesn't make sense to keep the two lots as a park. Instead, the best use for the property is for building single family residences.

 They announced that the lots would be put up for auction that fall.

After all the time, energy, and money expended by all parties, the state decided to <u>sell</u> the property for development! Does the term *hypocrite* come to mind? Hell, it gives the word *hypocrite* a bad name!

So, in November of 1993, the two infamous Lucas lots were sold to a developer for $730,000. It was a great buy. It was a huge public relations debacle for the South Carolina Coastal Council and all other like-minded organizations across the land. I hope it was also a wake-up call for the American public. I love these kinds of mistakes when they are made by the other side. This action by the state points out that this was not about the environment. It is really about power, money, and prestige. I was looking forward to showing my grand kids "the Lucas Environmental Park" on the shore. But, alas, it was not to be. Money came first to the state and it put the spotlight on the real issue. If they can't put the cost on the individual, then it ain't worth doing!

10
Conclusions

OR:

The Price of Liberty Is Eternal Vigilance and Then Go Do Something About It

God cleared His throat nervously as He rose to address the Board of Environmental Protection. His engineers had been working on the plans for the tides project for almost two-and-a-half years and the environmental impact statement (three volumes not counting appendices) was complete. But he knew the board's staff was hostile and the neighbors, in this case everyone in the world who owned coastal real estate, were violently opposed. They had organized a group called Coastal Residents Against Pollution—C.R.A.P. Audiborn and the Conservation Law foundation had intervened. Earth First, in a well attended press conference, had announced that *they were boycotting the process entirely, even if it were permitted. God felt He had to go forward, however, something had to be done with the oceans twice a day because of the gravitational effect of the moon. Having the water rise and fall along the coast seemed a reasonable solution.*

Most people now liked the moon, by the way, although there had been some opposition at first. The opposition had been based on the grounds of visual pollution of the night sky, you could not see the stars as well as before.

Friends of the Animals had also objected because of the unfair advantage the moon gave predators, like foxes and owls, that were after the rodents. Fortunately, Friends of the Predators had intervened and helped God out. Finally God settled the moon case by promising no more than one full moon a month and that it would be phased in at that. It had been a close call. The vote was 5 to 4, and the Board was getting tougher all the time.

God also had some financial pressure to go ahead, although He would never mention this to the Board. He had already spent two million dollars on the application, and He figured the only way of recouping any of that was to complete at least some part of the project. "We are aware there might be some unavoidable environmental effects from this project," God said, opening His prepared statement.

The several hundred members of C.R.A.P. in the audience, most of whom held signs which said things like "Tides In, God's Out" and "No Bathtub Ring for Our World," laughed derisively. Some hissed. Their attorney rolled his eyes. But God continued.

"Some such effect is inevitable if we are to maintain the moon in its present location. We tried to mitigate the problem by exaggerating the rise and fall in the extreme northern and southern latitudes and maximizing it around the equator, where the water is warmer and more hospitable."

"But what about the cost of building floating docks in places like Maine?" someone shouted from the back of the room. "And the smell every eight hours when all that mud and guck is exposed?" God winced. He was hoping that this point would not come up because it might generate air quality review. Another year of monitoring and more millions for consultants. Yes somebody else said, "What about erosion? Who is going to pay to shore up the foundation to my cottage?"

Some erosion at the edge of any water body is inevitable, God pointed out, while trying to stay calm. But his answer was lost in the chorus from the audience. Had He done a study of the effects of aquatic organisms? What about the wetlands? How would people figure out the intertidal zone? Where was the noise study?

Those waves coming in all night would make it impossible to sleep. What about the possible salt water effects on adjacent wells or impacts on seabird nesting patterns.

Quietly God folded His files and started to leave. Looking back at the Board, He saw they were arguing whether the public hearing schedule should be extended to include a few days in the Southern Hemisphere, and whether a solid waste issue was necessary because of the driftwood problem.

On His way out,...God bent down and whispered to His administrative assistant.

"Noah," He said, "I think I have another idea...."

Angus King's closing lines at the Lucas presentation 04/24/93 Bangor, Maine, taped at 4:30 P.M. by Carl Snow.

I often times end my speeches with the above story. I had to miss that particular meeting of MECRI (Maine Environmental Conservation Resources Institute] due to the death of my father that year. I have never met Mr. King, but I am indebted to him. The story is one that always elicits a good chuckle from my audience. They come up to me after my speech and say things like, "You know David, we are not too far away from that situation today in America." Sadly, I must agree.

In the past three years, I have continued to receive literally hundreds of telephone calls from people all over the United States, Canada, England, and even Australia. Each one of them have had a problem with a governmental body taking land unconstitutionally from them or a family member. Each and every one of them is as frustrated as God was in Angus's version of what really caused the heavenly flood.

Why is this? How did a country that was founded on private property and the freedom to use it, come to such a juncture in its history? Let me take a stab at answering that question.

I believe that there are three major categories of people and organizations in this country that think private property should take a back seat to their particular special interest. There are other categories and groups that I am sure you can add to my list. But here are my selections for your consideration.

The first and most obvious group is the so-called environmentalist. They are the most visible, the most vocal, the most successful, the best organized, and the most well-funded group responsible for cases of unconstitutional takings of private property. They are not, however, the only ones responsible for the growth of these uncompensated takings, but they have led the way.

The second group is the "no growth," or the "not in my backyard" group: the "Nimbys." These are the ones with what I call, "the draw bridge mentality." These folks would like to dig a moat around their town or city and pull up the drawbridge. They take the position that when they moved into their new community or city, it reached perfection at that exact moment. The community was somehow instantly transformed into the new and improved Garden of Eden with their arrival. Paradise reclaimed, so to speak.

The next family that attempts to move into this newly created utopia has the opposite effect and upsets this delicate perfection. They are, therefore, not welcome. They are in league with the devil and are trying to destroy this new Garden of Eden. "Pull up the draw bridge, no more people," they shout. Included in this category are the preservationists. They believe that everything old is better than anything new.

The third group of people that I have in mind, have been around for a long, long time. They are the socialists and communists who believe that our entire system of private property is immoral and wrong. Private property should not exist. Most Americans think that just because the Soviet Union failed, the Utopia of Communism has been forever discredited. I ask you to think again, my fellow citizens. Nothing is further from the truth. These

American social engineers want to do for America what the social engineers of the failed Soviet Union did for Russia. They arrogantly and even sometimes sincerely believe that they have greater insight into how property should be used than you or I do. These land planning socialists feel morally and intellectually superior to average Americans and therefore justified in doing whatever it takes to implement their vision of how things should be.

Apologists from all over the world are already shifting the blame for the failure of that system to other causes and not to the ideas of brothers Marx, Engels, and Lenin. These rewriters of history will tell you that perhaps it was Stalin, and the other mass murderers that the system produced, that perverted it. Or, they will say, that it was creeping capitalism that ruined the pure ideals of the communist/socialist order. You should remember that the basic tenet of communism is the "abolition of private property." That is the principle reason the communist/socialist system failed.

The joint efforts of these three special interest groups have had a devastating effect on the lives of millions of Americans; effects that are not always clear and tangible even to the people involved in the private property rights movement. Let us begin with the so-called environmentalist group. In 1967, I was a sophomore at the University of South Carolina. That summer, I went on an adventure. I traveled to Alaska to find a summer job. I had heard the call of the wild and wanted to see that great state.

I got a job as a game warden in the Sitka district of Southeastern Alaska. I was hired to protect the annual salmon runs that returned to Alaskan waters to spawn. I returned every summer until 1970. I saw the Alaskan wilderness up close and put my life on the line in helping to protect those magnificent natural resources and wildlife. I made several arrests of game law violators during my summers there.

Being an avid fisherman and hunter, I have more recently participated in building impoundments for waterfowl, planting food plots for game management, restocking wild turkeys on my own property, and improving the nesting habitat for songbirds on my farm in Lee County, South Carolina.

I am also an experienced scuba diver and have enjoyed under- water contact with mother nature. This activity encouraged me to join Jacque Cousteau's organization to "help preserve our under water wonders." I have reconsidered my membership in light of some of the things that I have found out during my recent ordeal.

The point of all of this is that I consider myself

to be as much of an environmentalist as anyone. That is not what the fight is about. It has become a fight over the old issues of freedom, money, power, and control.

In the 1950s, President Eisenhower warned America to beware of what he called the Military-Industrial Complex. The idea that arms makers influence government decisions was nothing new. What was new was the term that the President used to describe the theory.

Ike told us that there were groups that benefited from world strife, tension, and yes, even war. The arms makers made money selling armaments, munitions, goods, and services. The government bureaucrats benefited from the enhanced power and ever increasing military budgets given to them. This was considered by many to be an unholy and very dangerous arrangement.

Today, the same people who readily endorsed the profit motive for the members of the Military-Industrial Complex turn a blind eye to the dangers of the environmental-government-complex or "the Green Machine." This manevolent axis between government and environmental groups has become very wealthy and powerful during the last thirty years.

This Green Machine is comprised of lawyers looking for fees; professors looking for grants; consultants looking for contracts; specialists looking for new ecological problems that they can then be paid to solve; marketing people looking for ways to sell "green approved" products; manufacturers producing environmentally safe new projects; big business looking to eliminate competition and enhance profits; doctors and drug manufacturers pushing new fad diets, pills or treatments; bureaucrats wanting to be promoted; politicians running for lifetime offices; elitists trying to make you do what they know is best for you; activists raising money for their organizations; and the list goes on and on. The more complex that they can make and issue seem, the more it benefits their particular profession and magnifies their own importance. When this oftentimes unwitting alliance is active in the private market, its effects are bad enough. When the government became a willing and active part of the Green Machine in order to extend its power into the public domain, then it has become an entity that is powerful indeed.

Big business cuts deal after deal trying to buy peace at any price with both the Green Machine. This is extortion on a grand scale. Small business and entrepreneurs on the other hand, go out of business fighting the mountains of new rules and regulations. Outspoken leaders of the green movement are moving into jobs throughout federal, state, and local governments.

Their Mafia-like tactics are fear, publicity, political action, more fear, more publicity, then more political action. It has been a surefire money and power getter for a long time. The main environmental groups bring in over 2.6 billion dollars each year in donations. This only begins the equation. Next, factor in federal, state, and local governmental departments that are involved with the environment.

With billions more in dollars, almost unlimited manpower, and of course, the power of the gun (law enforcement), they have been able to radically tilt public opinion and power in their direction. They are also empowered by the national news media, and that's no small advantage. In addition to the above, thousands of companies have sprung up to take advantage of the new environmental industry. They have a big stake in the new "Green Machine" as well. They provide research, products, and experts to fuel the spread of the power of the "Green Machine." This group would make the Krupp Armaments people blush with shame. They frighten people not just in their home country, but people all over the world. Chicken Little is now told not that the sky is falling, but that it is being destroyed. There will be no sky left to fall.

There are serious problems in areas of the environment, but the Green Machine does not benefit from real solutions to real problems. They increase their revenue by scaring the hell out of people. The bigger the crisis, the bigger the donations.

Under close scientific scrutiny, most of these manufactured crises are not crises after all. By the time serious science has looked over the problem, it is usually too late. Laws have been passed in a rush to be the most caring, the most compassionate, and the most politically correct.

The situation reminds me of the time my brother Stephen and I were working with a young three year old colt. Steve was breaking him to saddle. The colt's name is Desert Sword. He is a beautiful, dark bay, Egyptian Arabian, and very smart. We had him tied to the wall, and were in the process of putting the saddle on him, when brother Steve and I made a mistake.

The saddle girth got kinked up on the opposite side of the colt. Instead of unbuckling the cinch before we retied the saddle, we decided to take a short cut. We left the saddle loosely tied on the horse's back.

Steve ducked under the horse's neck to straighten out the kink. Sword shied and the saddle slipped under his stomach. Since the saddle was still buckled it didn't fall off, the colt panicked and jerked the chain out of the wall. Steve and I dove for the door of the stall and made it out just before all hell broke loose. Round and round the stall went Sword. He was bucking, kicking, and falling down. We were finally able to stop him before he hurt himself and tore up the saddle.

The horse was frightened by something that he didn't understand. He panicked, nearly injured himself, my brother and me, and he ruined the equipment—all because he panicked. Our government is like that. At the slightest perceived threat, they go into the same kind of motion that the horse did. Only we are not as lucky at getting out of harm's way and saving our property as my brother and I were with my horse.

Usually, there is great damage done before we realize that the cure is much worse than the original problem. Each time somebody's saddle slips, off goes our government with half baked laws and rules that cost billions of dollars in taxpayer's money, to cure a problem that could best be handled in a simpler, less intrusive manner. Our government needs to learn to act more responsibly. Ah, but perhaps there is too much profit at stake to simply solve a problem without creating hundreds more.

I have been asked by many people if I think we will ever reach a balance in this country between environmentalists and private property. My answer is that as long as ignorance and fear continue to bring in donations and win elections, these groups will continue to be professional fearmongers.

I can picture in my mind the day that the staff of the Sierra Club's New York office addresses the last meeting of the board of directors.

"Ladies, and Gentlemen of the Board. It is with great pleasure that we announce to you that we are no longer needed. All major environmental problems have been solved. Spaceship Earth is now safe, along with all of its endangered species and ecosystems. With your help and direction we have attained all of our objectives.

The last group of the most wanted environmental criminals have been hunted down, rounded up and executed. Therefore we propose shutting down our operations except for a skeleton crew and returning the twelve million dollars left in our bank accounts to our donors. We do not need to collect our usual forty to fifty million per year in donations. We can now keep a watchful eye on things for only a million or two."

It won't happen. As long as the Green Machine can literally frighten people out of their money, frighten them they will. Al Capone should have taken lessons from these guys. This government locks up the victims and not the thieves. How clever.

This group has led the way for the " Nimbys," or "the not in my back yard crowd." They have passed law after law that takes property through regulation without paying for it. And at the time, it even seems justified under the circumstances of fear and ignorance foisted upon the public.

The " Nimbys" support tough zoning laws to keep their community the way they like it. They use zoning, not as a tool to promote orderly growth, but to stop it all together. If the Green Machine can restrict property and not pay for it, then they can do the same thing.

Zoning used sparingly, and with sensitivity to property rights, can be a useful land planning tool. But used unconstitutionally to take property, it becomes a nightmare for millions of American property owners. In November of 1993, the city of Houston, Texas held a special election. The city did not have zoning, but the bureaucrats wanted the power that it would bring. The people of Houston listened carefully to both sides and voted sixty-six percent against zoning.

Here is one of the finest cities in the world, and it gets along great without zoning. To listen to zoning proponents, the entire system would collapse without it. The people of Houston are doing just fine. Zoning today, is really about something else, prejudice. It is used to exclude undesirable elements from society. It is the old European ghetto system under a more benign name.

A fine example of this at work is found right here in my state of South Carolina. In the early 1950s the island of Hilton Head was home to poverty, disease, and despair. The population was mostly black and had been isolated since the island was settled in the 1770s. But Hilton Head also had some of the best beaches in the world. Along comes a young man named Charles Fraser. His family owned lots of timberland on Hilton Head.

Mr. Fraser changed Hilton Head and the state of South Carolina with an idea. The Sea Pines Resort was born. Wealthy people began building and buying homes there. Jobs became plentiful. The price of land rose dramatically. Fortunes were made and lost. Economic opportunity came to people who would not have had it otherwise. Today, poverty, disease, and hunger are very rare things on Hilton Head island.

So now the newly incorporate city administration on Hilton Head has stated that no new development is needed. Stop progress, stop economic prosperity, stop change, that is the message. All of those wealthy people will still be wealthy, but guess what? Many of the remaining landowners are poor and disadvantaged who have owned property for generations and who are now poised to finally participate in making real money in the private sector.

Sorry, but the power structure is stopping progress. The economic ladder is being pulled up. No one else will be allowed to climb it. That is, unless you are connected. Then, of course, things can be arranged. But it seems that only big companies with lots of money get to play in those "arranged" circumstances. They can't take chances on some little guy trying to become a big guy.

I have often wondered what the no-growth people say to the fact that most of the things that they are trying to save or preserve got that way because there weren't any "no-growth" people around to stop the builders. Take any great city in the world. They all became great through growth. Imagine trying to build one of the world's most beautiful cities, San Francisco, from scratch in today's restrictive climate. And, of course, is it suitable for human habitation, considering all of those earthquakes they have there?

How silly to try to stop the very engine that creates the thing people want to keep. Of course, I understand that a lot of people feel things have changed for the worse. I will bet you that my Cherokee ancestors would argue that things were better before the Europeans came here. But, how many would trade the modern world for the old one if the romance and illusion of the past were stripped away and what was left was a stone age existence with all of its dangers and lack of modern comforts?

The third group of people that support the suppression of private property rights is made up of socialists. They believe that the ownership of private property is just plain wrong. These people think that the free enterprise system is immoral. They advocate replacing our system with socialism. Even today, this centuries-old argument continues. Are the needs of society more important than the needs of the individual? Remember the director of the South Carolina Coastal Council, Wayne Beam's, comments about how sometimes the individual must sacrifice for the good of society?

This has been and will continue to be the focus of politics for all societies. I certainly do not think that in this short space, on this topic of private property rights, that I can instantly win this argument. After all, there is no one as blind as he who will not see. That said, I would like to restate the benefits that individual freedom of action brings to mankind.

Greatness is born of necessity, opportunity, and freedom. The freedom to act is the most important of these for achieving greatness. Every man or woman who accomplishes anything worthwhile was given or took for themselves, the freedom to act. The genius of America is that the American experiment has tried to give all of its citizens the freedom to achieve. It's known as the American Dream. The more freedom, the more greatness, the less freedom, the less greatness. Restraint stifles initiative. Less initiative means less accomplishment. This is clearly shown by the failure of socialism to compete with free enterprise systems.

Of course, freedom does not mean license to

do harm or be a nuisance to others. That is the primary purpose of our system of government: to arbitrate fairly between where freedom ends and nuisance begins. We are now engaged in a debate over just those issues.

The line drawn over two hundred years ago in the American constitution is being erased. Traditional uses for private property now fall prey to the false fears and maneuvers of ignorance and greed. More and more Americans are waking up to that fact. As they do, a counter attack is on the horizon. The justification for big government oppression is beginning to wear thin on many Americans.

The size of our government and its great power to do harm is being felt by its citizens now on a grand scale.

In response, organizations are springing up all across the nation to combat this growing menace to our hard won freedoms. People are finally beginning to question the growing power of this "Green Machine" that first steals from its citizens and imprisons them when they object and resist. Today there are over 1500 grass roots organizations. They are dedicated to protecting private property rights and all of the other freedoms that result from ownership of property. The total estimated membership of these property rights advocates is over twelve million.

In The United States Congress and in state legislatures around the country, politicians concerned that we are destroying the system that has created the highest standard of living in the history of mankind are working to reverse the damage. They understand that our system is being perverted for no other reason than old fashioned greed and a lust for power. This book has been about one battle that took place in this ancient fight for freedom. There are many others fought each day, between those who seek limits and restraints in order to control and those who seek freedom to achieve and live the American dream.

Today, in America, these three groups, along with government, our news media, and our educational systems are miring us in a circle of fear. They seek to use this fear to control, limit, and restrain our society.

Is there anything on earth more important to preserve than individual American liberty? Change will come to America and to the rest of the world with or without liberty. Look at history and judge which way is best.

Instead of this divisive negative approach to protecting the things that seem to be important to large segments of our society, I would like to see a more positive approach. The profit motive and individual self-interest has been the fuel that has always driven our society. I can guarantee that if a generous tax credit were to be extended to the protecting landowners of an endangered species, that's one problem that would be quickly solved. Just how quickly, would depend on how big the tax break. The money now spent on punitive enforcement of unconstitutional laws would do more good if used to entice and not to threaten. Americans historically don't cotton to threats. With all of the land owned by the federal government just compensation could perhaps take the form of a swap of assets or by selling off government land not considered critical to some program some where (if there is such a thing). Long term wildlife and plant easements could be paid for with tax breaks spread out over a reasonable time period. These tax breaks would be offset by shifting public funds from oppressive enforcement bureaucracies to environmental organization that are truly more concerned with solving problems than with creating new ones to raise fear funds.

On November 8, 1994, The American public woke up to the dangers facing them. They have elected a group of Senators, Congressmen, Governors, and state legislators who seemed determined to change the direction of our country. The private property movement was a major factor in electing these people to office. The road back to individual freedom is long and winding. Today there is hope that a new and better trail is being blazed by our leaders, and citizens. Private property protection must be recognized as the bedrock of all individual freedom. I hope for the day when we can truly say: "Each person can sit under his vine and his fig tree, and no one shall make him afraid."

David Lucas on his former beachfront property in 1995. Even though it was deemed unfit to build on, the property was at the time surrounded by expensive houses.

Epilogue

I wish that I could write "The End" at this point. It would be great news if you were reading this book in an ancient history class but sadly that is not the case. It now is May, 1995. The War over private property rights continues to rage. The good news is that the forces fighting to protect the rights that you have to own and use private property without undue and illegal interference from either private groups or meddling government bureaucrats seem to be winning a few victories.

The *Lucas* case, I believe, added to the arsenal of weapons that citizens can use to protect their private property rights. Several areas of law and policy, which influence the determination of "just compensation" paid to the property owner, were impacted positively by the High Court's ruling in *Lucas*. Specifically, these issues define what constitutes "a taking," "economically viable use" and the "nuisance" exception.

The issue of "ripeness" was also argued in this case. Those of you who have ever had to deal with the government in general, and the court system in particular, know that the time and expense involved in waiting for a court to even take your case is a major weapon used by the bureaucrats against property owners. I have met one man from Vermont who went all the way to the United States Supreme Court on a property rights case, only to have them rule that he had started in the wrong court. His case was therefore not "ripe." He was forced to start all over again. That was fourteen years ago, but he presses on doggedly.

Just how "ripe" does a case have to be? Rotten maybe? Or do you just have to be bankrupt before you are considered ripe enough? In our case, we won the very, very important ripeness issue. Justice Souter tried to worm out of deciding if a taking had occurred by trying to drag up the ripeness issue. He wrote a separate opinion stating that because of the ripeness he wanted the case sent back to the lower courts. Thank goodness Souter was alone in that position.

One of the most important points made by the *Lucas* case was that it settled the "takings" issue: Can a regulation be a taking. In *Pennsylva-*

nia Coal Co. V. Mahon Justice Oliver Wendel Homes stated that, "If a regulation goes too far, it will be considered a taking." That statement was made over seventy years ago. The Supreme Court found in the *Lucas* case, that finally, a government regulation had "gone too far" and was therefore a taking.

The Court also ruled that a total loss of value warrants a separate category of takings. If all "economically viably use" of property is restricted, then a taking has occurred and "just compensation" is owed. If less than all "economically viable use" is restricted then the courts are required to look further before finding a taking. Courts must examine the intent of the regulation and the "investment backed expectations" of the property owner to see if compensation is due.

Much was made of this one hundred percent distinction by the opponents of property rights. However, as mentioned earlier, Justice Scalia had admonished the public that the Court was not limiting a regulatory taking to only those cases in which there was a total loss of value. Several subsequent cases have shown that he meant what he said. See footnote number eight.

One other important area that was cleared up by the *Lucas* case is the "nuisance" issue raised by Justice Toal using the *Mugler* line of cases. Some earlier courts had interpreted the nuisance exception to include any law passed by the legislature that had a harm preventing purpose. The Court ruled that there is no difference between harm preventing and benefit bestowing. The only nuisance exception to the Fifth Amendment's takings clause is when the particular nuisance is pre-existing. In that instance the property would have no value because of the already existing nuisance. Otherwise the Court observed that figuring out if a law regulates only a nuisance boils down to whether or not the new law or regulation has "artful harm-preventing characterizations" by the staff of the General Assembly.

Lucas also threw the burden of proving whether or not the law regulates a nuisance back where it belongs, on the regulating entity and not on the property owner. The South Carolina Coastal Council tried unsuccessfully to prove that building houses on my lots was a nuisance. From now on, lawmakers around the nation will be forced to be very careful in writing new legislation dealing with restrictions on property usage. Laws must now be tailored to deal with a specific nuisance. Governments can no longer write broad laws that throw the baby out with the bath water. Of course, that is the way things should have been done all along. When governments now propose broad-based, land use regulations, they must be based on specific, pre-existing nuisances or the regulating entity must pay the compensation demanded by the Fifth Amendment.

Perhaps the most important thing to come out of all of this is hope for the future. Many Americans had seemingly given up on the system. It appeared to a lot of people that normal Americans no longer had access to a fair hearing. They felt that only the radical extremist benefitted from the system. It was as if the American government had fallen into the hands of radicals while we were all asleep. In a sense this was the truth. In a way *Lucas* was about whether average American citizens have a say in the matter of where our government is taking us. I have been amazed at the number of people who have fallen prey to the old saw that "you can't fight city hall." Well, you can. I did and I won. And even though it may seem self-evident, I did it within the system. That fact, in today's political climate of polarization, is a reaffirmation of the system that our Founding Fathers conceived for their descendants. The rights of average Americans still matter.

In the fall of 1993, I helped formed the Council on Property Rights. This is a national organization dedicated to protecting the takings clause of the Fifth Amendment. I had been touched by so many people and their problems that I felt that we had to continue to be involved in the fight to protect private property. Subsequently, the Council On Property Rights has been involved in drafting model private property protection legislation both on the national and the state level. The Council on Property Rights has joined with many other property rights organizations to network, exchange and coordinate information. We have testified in Congress and spent countless hours on the telephone helping people with their property rights problems. This takes the form of individual advice, introduction to some of the fine property rights legal services that are now available, or sometimes just offering encouragement and comfort.

Today, to fight for your property rights is expensive, time consuming, frustrating, lonesome, and without any guarantee of success. But the odds of success are improving. Many Public Interest Legal Services have emerged to meet the rising need of private property owners. If you need help and you can't reach me, then call one of these gallant groups of legal Lancelots to come to your rescue. A partial, but by no means exhaustive, list includes The Southeastern Legal Foundation in Atlanta, Georgia; Defenders of Property Rights, in Washington, D.C.; The Institute for Justice in Washington, D.C.; Mountain States Legal Foundation, in Denver, Colorado; and of course the Pacific Legal Foundation, in Sacramento, California.

But the most important point of all to remember is that the outcome of this struggle matters to you *and* to your children. Anytime anyone of us loses a right, we all lose one. I like to think that the **Lucas** case has motivated others to get involved. If you aren't involved yet, I ask that you do so now. Join my organization or one of the hundreds of others that have sprung up in response to the assault of the Green Machine on American liberties.

Since the **Lucas** decision was handed down in June of 1992, several other cases have added to the growing number of wins in the private property rights column. Dan Dolan and his courageous mother in the **Dolan** case, along with the **Florida Rock** case and the **Loveladies Harbor** case, have all recently advanced the protection of private property. These cases prove that the court has now recognized that a partial loss of value is now compensable just as a total loss was in the **Lucas** case. Remember footnote number eight.

Even with these additional victories, your property is not safe. The Green Machine has a mon-eyed motivation now to keep coming up with new environmental crises. They will find new victims to vilify and new ways to attack private property. I am not saying that the environment should be ignored. To the contrary, I believe in reasonable protection for our nation's environment. In addition, prudent planning for the future growth of our urban and suburban areas can, and does, add to their usefulness, enjoyability and value. I *am* saying that the constitution requires that if society wants your property for a public purpose, then society, or at least our American society must compensate the individual for his loss. The Fifth Amendment demands it, fairness demands it, justice demands it, and the American people are demanding it in a loud voice. After all, the Bill of Rights is there to protect us against just this kind of abuse of power by our own government.

There is a real need behind the creation of the Green Machine, just as there was real danger that justified the creation of the military-industrial complex. However, despite this, it became necessary to scrutinize the military-industrial complex because it oftentimes was self-serving and overstated dangers to justify more spending and an expansion of its power. We must now also use the same standards of scrutiny to examine the motives of the Green Machine. More often than not, the extremists in the Green Machine push crises, pseudo-scientific positions, legislation and/or regulations that benefit them personally. They benefit in either money, power, position or prestige. In some instances they gain from all of the above.

You must remember that The Green Machine is a multi-billion dollar industry. The Green Machine has become just another special interest group, with high paid, high profile and powerful lobbyists trying to promote its agenda at the expense of the American taxpayer and property owner. This struggle over property rights is no longer simply over what's best for the environment or even over "saving the environment." As is usual in this world, it is about money and power and no longer solely about the protection of the environment.

As soon as the Green Machine was successful in raising billions of dollars to "protect" the environment, every group involved with land use jumped on board and anything that could be couched in green terminology was deemed acceptable regardless of its real purpose. Well, as I found out the hard way, the Green Machine is made up of people motivated by self-interest, just like the rest of us. Some are well-intentioned individuals that believe with a religious devotion, but the power behind the Green Machine will never achieve sainthood, contrary to their self- promoting propaganda. If you follow the money trail, in most instances, you will find the answer to whether or not there is a real problem. Or, as often happens, will the next crisis result in a grant for millions of dollars to study the problem? Perhaps a promotion will result? Best of all, if it's scary enough millions of dollars in donations and thousands of new memberships will result. If that new project can be kept out of the neighborhoods, then competition will be reduced and those already present will be protected. Those protected businesses gain while the public pays and the property owner is ruined.

Much remains to be done. Legislation codifying the recent Supreme Court rulings needs to be enacted on the federal level and in every state in the Union. This protective legislation will result, not in the ruination of the environment, but in the protection of individual property rights. It will allow real and reasonable solutions to real environmental problems and, for a change, at a reasonable cost to the nation's economy. It will reveal to the American public, the hidden costs of radical and silly regulation that do not in fact, protect anything but the interest of the Green Machine. This will force a much needed discipline on groups too long used to having carte blanche for any program that is colored, or even tinged, with green.

Needless and wasteful litigation will be avoided and the funds and man-hours being wasted on this unconstitutional approach can be spent on positive solutions to problems. Today, instead, money is wasted on lawyers' fees, court costs, reduced value of assets, increased costs of all products, soaring taxes, loss of services, production delays and unnecessary administrative staffing (more bureaucrats). Productivity will increase. The economy will benefit from the redirection of the billions of dollars lost in unproductive, unsuccessful, wasteful and unconstitutional spending habits forced by the special interests of the Green Machine.

The Supreme Court has finally begun to enforce the takings clause of the Fifth Amendment. The House of Representatives has passed a"Takings" bill. The Senate will soon begin debate on their version of a "Takings" bill. Many states will follow suit. The benefits are many, the drawbacks are non-existent. Join a property rights organization and help us restore the integrity of private property in America. The fight for the natural rights of man continues as before. *You and you alone* will determine whether or not the American government remains a government of the people, by the people, and for the people. Or, if our government, like all those before it in history, becomes just another instrument of oppression instead of the beacon of freedom that it was conceived to be!

In 1773, Adam Smith, one of England's most outstanding Renaissance men and a close confidante and friend of Benjamin Franklin, wrote the now famous *Wealth of Nations*. He describes very eloquently our present day problem with many government activities. He wrote:

"Every individual, it is evident, can, in his local situation, judge much better than any statesman or lawgiver can do for him. The statesman who should attempt to direct private people in what manner they ought to employ their capitals would not only load himself with a most unnecessary attention, but assume an authority which could safely be trusted not only to no single person, but to no council or senate whatever, and which would no where be so dangerous as in the hands of a man who had folly and presumption enough to fancy himself fit to exercise it."

In the words of King Solomon, "There's nothing new under the sun."

P.S.—At the time of this writing, the state of South Carolina has refused to refund the property taxes that I was forced to pay while they had "Taken" my property. The never ending story of governments and their lust for taxes continues.

P.P.S.—May 4, 1995. I just walked down the beach and passed the lot where I was going to build my house in 1988. *Someone else has begun construction of their dream home!* Thanks for the memories, Jean baby.

P.P.P.S.—I have a new neighbor on the island. His name is *Cotton Harness, Esquire—the original attorney for the South Carolina Coastal Council*. His home is now closer to the beach than my present home is. Don't you love the way the truth slowly comes forth but only after the gate has been left opened and the mule has gotten away and the damage has been done!

APPENDIX I

OPINION

SUPREME COURT OF THE UNITED STATES

No. 91–453

DAVID H. LUCAS, PETITIONER *v.* SOUTH CAROLINA
COASTAL COUNCIL

ON WRIT OF CERTIORARI TO THE SUPREME COURT OF SOUTH CAROLINA

[June 29, 1992]

JUSTICE SCALIA delivered the opinion of the Court.

In 1986, petitioner David H. Lucas paid $975,000 for two
residential lots on the Isle of Palms in Charleston County, South
Carolina, on which he intended to build single- family homes.
In 1988, however, the South Carolina Legislature enacted the
Beachfront Management Act, S.C. Code §48–39–250 *et seq.*
(Supp. 1990) (Act), which had the direct effect of barring
petitioner from erecting any permanent habitable structures
on his two parcels. See §48–39– 290(A). A state trial court
found that this prohibition rendered Lucas's parcels "valueless."
App. to Pet. for Cert. 37. This case requires us to decide whether
the Act's dramatic effect on the economic value of Lucas's lots
accomplished a taking of private property under the Fifth and
Fourteenth Amendments requiring the payment of "just
compensation." U. S. Const., Amdt. 5.

South Carolina's expressed interest in intensively managing
development activities in the so-called "coastal zone" dates from
1977 when, in the aftermath of Congress's passage of the federal
Coastal Zone Management Act of 1972, 86 Stat. 1280, as
amended, 16 U. S. C. §1451 *et seq.*, the legislature enacted a

LUCAS VS. THE GREEN MACHINE

Coastal Zone Management Act of its own. See S. C. Code §48–39–10 *et seq.* (1987). In its original form, the South Carolina Act required owners of coastal zone land that qualified as a "critical area" (defined in the legislation to include beaches and immediately adjacent sand dunes, §48–39–10(J)) to obtain a permit from the newly created South Carolina Coastal Council (respondent here) prior to committing the land to a "use other than the use the critical area was devoted to on [September 28, 1977]." §48–39–130(A).

In the late 1970's, Lucas and others began extensive residential development of the Isle of Palms, a barrier island situated eastward of the City of Charleston. Toward the close of the development cycle for one residential subdivision known as "Beachwood East," Lucas in 1986 purchased the two lots at issue in this litigation for his own account. No portion of the lots, which were located approximately 300 feet from the beach, qualified as a "critical area" under the 1977 Act; accordingly, at the time Lucas acquired these parcels, he was not legally obliged to obtain a permit from the Council in advance of any development activity. His intention with respect to the lots was to do what the owners of the immediately adjacent parcels had already done: erect single-family residences. He commissioned architectural drawings for this purpose.

The Beachfront Management Act brought Lucas's plans to an abrupt end. Under that 1988 legislation, the Council was directed to establish a "baseline" connecting the landward-most "point[s] of erosion . . . during the past forty years" in the region of the Isle of Palms that includes Lucas's lots. §48–39–280(A)(2) (Supp. 1988).[1] In action not challenged here, the Council fixed this baseline landward of Lucas's parcels. That was significant, for under the Act construction of occupable improvements[2] was flatly prohibited seaward of a line drawn 20 feet landward of, and parallel to, the baseline, §48–39–290(A) (Supp. 1988). The Act provided no exceptions.

Lucas promptly filed suit in the South Carolina Court of Common Pleas, contending that the Beachfront Management Act's construction bar effected a taking of his property withoutjust compensation. Lucas did not take issue with the validity of the Act as a lawful exercise of South Carolina's police power, but contended that the Act's complete extinguishment of his property's value entitled him to compensation regardless of whether the legislature had acted in furtherance of legitimate police power objectives. Following a bench trial, the court agreed. Among its factual determinations was the finding that "at the time Lucas purchased the two lots, both were zoned for single-family residential construction and . . . there were no restrictions imposed upon such use of the property by either the State of South Carolina, the County of Charleston, or the Town of the Isle of Palms." App. to Pet. for Cert. 36. The trial court further found that the Beachfront Management Act decreed a permanent ban on construction insofar as Lucas's lots were concerned, and that this prohibition "deprive[d] Lucas of any reasonable economic use of the lots, . . . eliminated the unrestricted right of use, and render[ed] them valueless." *Id.*, at 37. The court thus concluded that Lucas's properties had been "taken" by operation of the Act, and it ordered respondent to pay "just compensation" in the amount of $1,232,387.50. *Id.*, at 40.

The Supreme Court of South Carolina reversed. It found dispositive what it described as Lucas's concession "that the Beachfront Management Act [was] properly and validly designed to preserve . . . South Carolina's beaches." 304 S. C. 376, 379, 404 S. E. 2d 895, 896 (1991). Failing an attack on the validity of the statute as such, the court believed itself bound to accept the "uncontested . . . findings" of the South Carolina legislature that new construction in the coastal zone—such as petitioner intended—threatened this public resource. *Id.*, at 383, 404 S. E. 2d, at 898. The Court ruled that when a regulation respecting the use of property is designed "to prevent serious public harm," *id.*, at 383, 404 S. E. 2d, at 899 (citing, *inter alia, Mugler* v. *Kansas*, 123 U. S. 623 (1887)), no compensation is owing under the Takings Clause regardless of the regulation's effect on the property's value.

Two justices dissented. They acknowledged that our *Mugler* line of cases recognizes governmental power to prohibit "noxious" uses of property—*i.e.*, uses of property akin to "public nuisances"—without having to pay compensation. But they would not have characterized the Beachfront Management Act's *"primary* purpose [as] the prevention of a nuisance." 304 S. C., at 395, 404 S. E. 2d, at 906 (Harwell, J., dissenting). To the dissenters, the chief purposes of the legislation, among them the promotion of tourism and the creation of a "habitat for indigenous flora and fauna," could not fairly be compared to nuisance abatement. *Id.*, at 396, 404 S. E. 2d, at 906. As a consequence, they would have affirmed the trial court's conclusion that the Act's obliteration of the value of petitioner's lots accomplished a taking.

We granted certiorari. 502 U. S. ___ (1991).

As a threshold matter, we must briefly address the Council's suggestion that this case is inappropriate for plenary review. After briefing and argument before the South Carolina Supreme Court, but prior to issuance of that court's opinion, the Beachfront Management Act was amended to authorize the Council, in certain circumstances, to issue "special permits" for the construction or reconstruction of habitable structures seaward of the baseline. See S. C. Code §48–39–290(D)(1) (Supp. 1991). According to the Council, this amendment renders Lucas's claim of a permanent deprivation unripe, as Lucas may yet be able to secure permission to build on his property. "[The Court's] cases," we are reminded, "uniformly reflect an insistence on knowing the nature and extent of permitted development before adjudicating the constitutionality of the regulations that purport to limit it." *MacDonald, Sommer & Frates* v. *County of Yolo*, 477 U. S. 340, 351 (1986). See also *Agins* v. *Tiburon*, 447 U. S. 255, 260 (1980). Because petitioner "has not yet obtained a final decision regarding how [he] will be allowed to develop [his] property," *Williamson County Regional Planning Comm'n of Johnson City* v. *Hamilton Bank*, 473 U. S. 172, 190 (1985), the Council argues that he is not yet entitled to definitive adjudication of his takings claim in this Court.

We think these considerations would preclude review had

the South Carolina Supreme Court rested its judgment on ripeness grounds, as it was (essentially) invited to do by the Council, see Brief for Respondent 9, n. 3. The South Carolina Supreme Court shrugged off the possibility of further administrative and trial proceedings, however, preferring to dispose of Lucas's takings claim on the merits. Compare, *e.g.*, *San Diego Gas & Electric Co.*, 450 U. S. 621, 631–632 (1981). This unusual disposition does not preclude Lucas from applying for a permit under the 1990 amendment for *future* construction, and challenging, on takings grounds, any denial. But it does preclude, both practically and legally, any takings claim with respect to Lucas's *past* deprivation, *i. e.*, for his having been denied construction rights during the period before the 1990 amendment. See generally *First English Evangelical Lutheran Church of Glendale* v. *County of Los Angeles*, 482 U. S. 304 (1987) (holding that temporary deprivations of use are compensable under the Takings Clause). Without even so much as commenting upon the consequences of the South Carolina Supreme Court's judgment in this respect, the Council insists that permitting Lucas to press his claim of a past deprivation on this appeal would be improper, since "the issues of whether and to what extent [Lucas] has incurred a temporary taking . . . have simply never been addressed." Brief for Respondent 11. Yet Lucas had no reason to proceed on a "temporary taking" theory at trial, or even to seek remand for that purpose prior to submission of the case to the South Carolina Supreme Court, since as the Act then read, the taking was unconditional and permanent. Moreover, given the breadth of the South Carolina Supreme Court's holding and judgment, Lucas would plainly be unable (absent our intervention now) to obtain further state-court adjudication with respect to the 1988–1990 period.

In these circumstances, we think it would not accord with sound process to insist that Lucas pursue the late-created "special permit" procedure before his takings claim can be considered ripe. Lucas has properly alleged Article III injury-in-fact in this case, with respect to both the pre-1990 and post-1990 constraints placed on the use of his parcels by the Beachfront Management Act.[3] That there is a discretionary "special permit" procedure by which he may regain—for the future, at least—beneficial use of his land goes only to the prudential "ripeness" of Lucas's challenge, and for the reasons discussed we do not think it prudent to apply that prudential requirement here. See *Esposito* v. *South Carolina Coastal Council*, 939 F. 2d 165, 168 (CA4 1991), cert. pending, No. 91–941.[4] We leave for decision on remand, of course, the questions left unaddressed by the South Carolina Supreme Court as a consequence of its categorical disposition.[5]

Prior to Justice Holmes' exposition in *Pennsylvania Coal Co.* v. *Mahon*, 260 U. S. 393 (1922), it was generally thought that the Takings Clause reached only a "direct appropriation" of property, *Legal Tender Cases*, 12 Wall. 457, 551 (1871), or the functional equivalent of a "practical ouster of [the owner's] possession." *Transportation Co.* v. *Chicago*, 99 U. S. 635, 642 (1879). See also *Gibson* v. *United States*, 166 U. S. 269, 275–276 (1897). Justice Holmes recognized in *Mahon*, however, that if the protection against physical appropriations of private property was to be meaningfully enforced, the government's power to redefine the range of interests included in the ownership of property was necessarily constrained by constitutional limits. 260 U. S., at 414–415. If, instead, the uses of private property were subject to unbridled, uncompensated qualification under the police power, "the natural tendency of human nature [would be] to extend the qualification more and more until at last private property disappear[ed]." *Id.*, at 415. These considerations gave birth in that case to the oft-cited maxim that, "while property may be regulated to a certain extent, if regulation goes too far it will be recognized as a taking." *Ibid.*

Nevertheless, our decision in *Mahon* offered little insight into when, and under what circumstances, a given regulation would be seen as going "too far" for purposes of the Fifth Amendment. In 70-odd years of succeeding "regulatory takings" jurisprudence, we have generally eschewed any "'set formula'" for determining how far is too far, preferring to "engag[e] in... essentially ad hoc, factual inquiries," *Penn Central*

Transportation Co. v. *New York City*, 438 U. S. 104, 124 (1978) (quoting *Goldblatt* v. *Hempstead*, 369 U. S. 590, 594 (1962)). See Epstein, Takings: Descent and Resurrection, 1987 Sup. Ct. Rev. 1, 4. We have, however, described at least two discrete categories of regulatory action as compensable without case-specific inquiry into the public interest advanced in support of the restraint. The first encompasses regulations that compel the property owner to suffer a physical "invasion" of his property. In general (at least with regard to permanent invasions), no matter how minute the intrusion, and no matter how weighty the public purpose behind it, we have required compensation. For example, in *Loretto* v. *Teleprompter Manhattan CATV Corp.*, 458 U. S. 419 (1982), we determined that New York's law requiring landlords to allow television cable companies to emplace cable facilities in their apartment buildings constituted a taking, *id.*, at 435–440, even though the facilities occupied at most only 1½ cubic feet of the landlords' property, see *id.*, at 438, n. 16. See also *United States* v. *Causby*, 328 U. S. 256, 265, and n. 10 (1946) (physical invasions of airspace); cf. *Kaiser Aetna* v. *United States*, 444 U. S. 164 (1979) (imposition of navigational servitude upon private marina).

The second situation in which we have found categorical treatment appropriate is where regulation denies all economically beneficial or productive use of land. See *Agins*, 447 U. S., at 260; see also *Nollan* v. *California Coastal Comm'n*, 483 U. S. 825, 834 (1987); *Keystone Bituminous Coal Assn.* v. *DeBenedictis*, 480 U. S. 470, 495 (1987); *Hodel* v. *Virginia Surface Mining & Reclamation Assn., Inc.*, 452 U. S. 264, 295–296 (1981).[6] As we have said on numerous occasions, the Fifth Amendment is violated when land-use regulation "does not substantially advance legitimate state interests *or denies an owner economically viable use of his land.*" *Agins, supra*, at 260 (citations omitted) (emphasis added).[7]

We have never set forth the justification for this rule. Perhaps it is simply, as Justice Brennan suggested, that total deprivation of beneficial use is, from the landowner's point of view, the equivalent of a physical appropriation. See *San Diego*

Gas & Electric Co. v. *San Diego*, 450 U. S., at 652 (Brennan, J., dissenting). "[F]or what is the land but the profits thereof[?]" 1 E. Coke, Institutes ch. 1, §1 (1st Am. ed. 1812). Surely, at least, in the extraordinary circumstance when *no* productive or economically beneficial use of land is permitted, it is less realistic to indulge our usual assumption that the legislature is simply "adjusting the benefits and burdens of economic life," *Penn Central Transportation Co.*, 438 U. S., at 124, in a manner that secures an "average reciprocity of advantage" to everyone concerned. *Pennsylvania Coal Co.* v. *Mahon*, 260 U. S., at 415. And the *functional* basis for permitting the government, by regulation, to affect property values without compensation—that "Government hardly could go on if to some extent values incident to property could not be diminished without paying for every such change in the general law," *id.*, at 413—does not apply to the relatively rare situations where the government has deprived a landowner of all economically beneficial uses.

On the other side of the balance, affirmatively supporting a compensation requirement, is the fact that regulations that leave the owner of land without economically beneficial or productive options for its use—typically, as here, by requiring land to be left substantially in its natural state—carry with them a heightened risk that private property is being pressed into some form of public service under the guise of mitigating serious public harm. See, *e.g.*, *Annicelli* v. *South Kingstown*, 463 A. 2d 133, 140–141 (R.I. 1983) (prohibition on construction adjacent to beach justified on twin grounds of safety and "conservation of open space"); *Morris County Land Improvement Co.* v. *Parsippany-Troy Hills Township*, 40 N. J. 539, 552–553, 193 A. 2d 232, 240 (1963) (prohibition on filling marshlands imposed in order to preserve region as water detention basin and create wildlife refuge). As Justice Brennan explained: "From the government's point of view, the benefits flowing to the public from preservation of open space through regulation may be equally great as from creating a wildlife refuge through formal condemnation or increasing electricity production through a dam project that floods private property." *San Diego Gas & Elec. Co., supra*, at 652 (Brennan, J., dissenting). The many statutes on the books, both state and federal, that provide for the use of eminent domain to impose servitudes on private scenic lands preventing developmental uses, or to acquire such lands altogether, suggest the practical equivalence in this setting of negative regulation and appropriation. See, *e.g.*, 16 U. S. C. §410ff-1(a) (authorizing acquisition of "lands, waters, or interests [within Channel Islands National Park] (including but not limited to scenic easements)"); §460aa-2(a) (authorizing acquisition of "any lands, or lesser interests therein, including mineral interests and scenic easements" within Sawtooth National Recreation Area); §§ 3921–3923 (authorizing acquisition of wetlands); N. C. Gen. Stat. §113A-38 (1990) (authorizing acquisition of, *inter alia*, "'scenic easements'" within the North Carolina natural and scenic rivers system); Tenn. Code Ann. §§11– 15–101 — 11–15–108 (1987) (authorizing acquisition of "protective easements" and other rights in real property adjacent to State's historic, architectural, archaeological, or cultural resources).

We think, in short, that there are good reasons for our frequently expressed belief that when the owner of real property has been called upon to sacrifice *all* economically beneficial uses in the name of the common good, that is, to leave his property economically idle, he has suffered a taking.[8]

The trial court found Lucas's two beachfront lots to have been rendered valueless by respondent's enforcement of the coastal-zone construction ban.[9] Under Lucas's theory of the case, which rested upon our "no economically viable use" statements, that finding entitled him to compensation. Lucas believed it unnecessary to take issue with either the purposes behind the Beachfront Management Act, or the means chosen by the South Carolina Legislature to effectuate those purposes. The South Carolina Supreme Court, however, thought otherwise. In its view, the Beachfront Management Act was no ordinary enactment, but involved an exercise of South Carolina's "police powers" to mitigate the harm to the public interest that petitioner's use of his land might occasion. 304 S. C., at 384, 404 S. E. 2d, at 899. By neglecting to dispute the findings enumerated in the Act[10] or otherwise to challenge the legislature's purposes, petitioner "concede[d] that the beach/dune area of South Carolina's shores is an extremely valuable public resource; that the erection of new construction, *inter alia*, contributes to the erosion and destruction of this public resource; and that discouraging new construction in close proximity to the beach/dune area is necessary to prevent a great public harm." *Id.*, at 382–383, 404 S. E. 2d, at 898. In the court's view, these concessions brought petitioner's challenge within a long line of this Court's cases sustaining against Due Process and Takings Clause challenges the State's use of its "police powers" to enjoin a property owner from activities akin to public nuisances. See *Mugler* v. *Kansas*, 123 U. S. 623 (1887) (law prohibiting manufacture of alcoholic beverages); *Hadacheck* v. *Sebastian*, 239 U. S. 394 (1915) (law barring operation of brick mill in residential area); *Miller* v. *Schoene*, 276 U. S. 272 (1928) (order to destroy diseased cedar trees to prevent infection of nearby orchards); *Goldblatt* v. *Hempstead*, 369 U. S. 590 (1962) (law effectively preventing continued operation of quarry in residential area).

It is correct that many of our prior opinions have suggested that "harmful or noxious uses" of property may be proscribed by government regulation without the requirement of compensation. For a number of reasons, however, we think the South Carolina Supreme Court was too quick to conclude that that principle decides the present case. The "harmful or noxious uses" principle was the Court's early attempt to describe in theoretical terms why government may, consistent with the Takings Clause, affect property values by regulation without incurring an obligation to compensate—a reality we nowadays acknowledge explicitly with respect to the full scope of the State's police power. See, *e.g.*, *Penn Central Transportation Co.*, 438 U. S., at 125 (where State "reasonably conclude[s] that `the health, safety, morals, or general welfare' would be promoted by prohibiting particular contemplated uses of land," compensation need not accompany prohibition); see also *Nollan* v. *California Coastal Commission*, 483 U. S., at 834–835 ("Our cases have not elaborated on the standards for determining what constitutes a ʼlegitimate state interest[,]ʼ [but] [t]hey have made clear . . . that a broad range of governmental purposes and regulations satisfy these requirements"). We made this very point in *Penn Central Transportation Co.*, where, in the course of sustaining New York City's landmarks preservation program against a takings challenge, we rejected the petitioner's sugges-

tion that *Mugler* and the cases following it were premised on, and thus limited by, some objective conception of "noxiousness": "[T]he uses in issue in *Hadacheck*, *Miller*, and *Goldblatt* were perfectly lawful in themselves. They involved no ʼblameworthiness, . . . moral wrongdoing or conscious act of dangerous risk-taking which induce[d society] to shift the cost to a pa[rt]icular individual.ʼ Sax, Takings and the Police Power, 74 Yale L. J. 36, 50 (1964). These cases are better understood as resting not on any supposed ʼnoxiousʼ quality of the prohibited uses but rather on the ground that the restrictions were reasonably related to the implementation of a policy— not unlike historic preservation—expected to produce a widespread public benefit and applicable to all similarly situated property." 438 U. S., at 133–134, n. 30.

"Harmful or noxious use" analysis was, in other words, simply the progenitor of our more contemporary statements that "land-use regulation does not effect a taking if it ʼsubstantially advance[s] legitimate state interestsʼ . . . ." *Nollan, supra*, at 834 (quoting *Agins* v. *Tiburon*, 447 U. S., at 260); see also *Penn Central Transportation Co., supra*, at 127; *Euclid* v. *Ambler Realty Co.*, 272 U. S. 365, 387–388 (1926).

The transition from our early focus on control of "noxious" uses to our contemporary understanding of the broad realm within which government may regulate without compensation was an easy one, since the distinction between "harm-preventing" and "benefit-conferring" regulation is often in the eye of the beholder. It is quite possible, for example, to describe in *either* fashion the ecological, economic, and aesthetic concerns that inspired the South Carolina legislature in the present case. One could say that imposing a servitude on Lucas's land is necessary in order to prevent his use of it from "harming" South Carolina's ecological resources; or, instead, in order to achieve the "benefits" of an ecological preserve.[11] Compare, *e.g.*, *Claridge* v. *New Hampshire Wetlands Board*, 125 N.H. 745, 752, 485 A.2d 287, 292 (1984) (owner may, without compensation, be barred from filling wetlands because landfilling would deprive adjacent coastal habitats and marine fisheries of ecological support), with, *e.g.*, *Bartlett* v. *Zoning Comm'n of Old Lyme*, 161 Conn. 24, 30, 282 A. 2d 907, 910 (1971) (owner barred from filling tidal marshland must be compensated, despite municipality's "laudable" goal of "preserv[ing] marshlands from encroachment or destruction"). Whether one or the other of the competing characterizations will come to one's lips in a particular case depends primarily upon one's evaluation of the worth of competing uses of real estate. See Restatement (Second) of Torts §822, Comment *g*, p. 112 (1979) ("[p]ractically all human activities unless carried on in a wilderness interfere to some extent with others or involve some risk of interference"). A given restraint will be seen as mitigating "harm" to the adjacent parcels or securing a "benefit" for them, depending upon the observer's evaluation of the relative importance of the use that the restraint favors. See Sax, Takings and the Police Power, 74 Yale L. J. 36, 49 (1964) ("[T]he problem [in this area] is not one of noxiousness or harm-creating activity at all; rather it is a problem of inconsistency between perfectly innocent and independently desirable uses"). Whether Lucas's construction of single-family residences on his parcels should be described as bringing "harm" to South Carolina's adjacent ecological resources thus depends principally upon whether the describer believes that the State's use interest in nurturing those resources is so important that *any* competing adjacent use must yield.[12]

When it is understood that "prevention of harmful use" was merely our early formulation of the police power justification necessary to sustain (without compensation) *any* regulatory diminution in value; and that the distinction between regulation that "prevents harmful use" and that which "confers benefits" is difficult, if not impossible, to discern on an objective, value-free basis; it becomes self-evident that noxious-use logic cannot serve as a touchstone to distinguish regulatory "takings"—which require compensation—from regulatory deprivations that do not require compensation. *A fortiori* the legislature's recitation of a noxious-use justification cannot be the basis for departing from our categorical rule that total regulatory takings must be compensated. If it were, departure would virtually always be allowed. The South Carolina Supreme Court's approach would essentially nullify *Mahon*'s affirmation of limits to the noncompensable exercise of the police power. Our cases provide no support for this: None of them that employed the logic of "harmful use" prevention to sustain a regulation involved an allegation that the regulation wholly eliminated the value of the claimant's land. See *Keystone Bituminous Coal Assn.*, 480 U. S., at 513–514 (REHNQUIST, C.J., dissenting).[13]

Where the State seeks to sustain regulation that deprives land of all economically beneficial use, we think it may resist compensation only if the logically antecedent inquiry into the nature of the owner's estate shows that the proscribed use interests were not part of his title to begin with.[14] This accords, we think, with our "takings" jurisprudence, which has traditionally been guided by the understandings of our citizens regarding the content of, and the State's power over, the "bundle of rights" that they acquire when they obtain title to property. It seems to us that the property owner necessarily expects the uses of his property to be restricted, from time to time, by various measures newly enacted by the State in legitimate exercise of its police powers; "[a]s long recognized, some values are enjoyed under an implied limitation and must yield to the police power." *Pennsylvania Coal Co.* v. *Mahon*, 260 U. S., at 413. And in the case of personal property, by reason of the State's traditionally high degree of control over commercial dealings, he ought to be aware of the possibility that new regulation might even render his property economically worthless (at least if the property's only economically productive use is sale or manufacture for sale), see *Andrus* v. *Allard*, 444 U. S. 51, 66–67 (1979) (prohibition on sale of eagle feathers). In the case of land, however, we think the notion pressed by the Council that title is somehow held subject to the "implied limitation" that the State may subsequently eliminate all economically valuable use is inconsistent with the historical compact recorded in the Takings Clause that has become part of our constitutional culture.[15]

Where "permanent physical occupation" of land is concerned, we have refused to allow the government to decree it anew (without compensation), no matter how weighty the asserted "public interests" involved, *Loretto* v. *Teleprompter Manhattan CATV Corp.*, 458 U. S., at 426—though we assuredly *would* permit the government to assert a permanent easement that was a pre-existing limitation upon the landowner's title. Compare *Scranton* v. *Wheeler*, 179 U. S. 141, 163 (1900) (interests of "riparian owner in the submerged lands . . . bordering on a public navigable water" held subject to Government's navigational servitude), with *Kaiser Aetna* v. *United States*, 444 U. S., at 178–180 (imposition of navigational servitude on marina created and rendered navigable at private expense held to constitute a taking). We believe similar treatment must be accorded confiscatory regulations, *i. e.*, regulations that prohibit all economically beneficial use of land: Any limitation so severe cannot be newly legislated or decreed (without compensation), but must inhere in the title itself, in the restrictions that background principles of the State's law of property and nuisance already place upon land ownership. A law or decree with such an effect must, in other words, do no more than duplicate the result that could have been achieved in the courts—by adjacent landowners (or other uniquely affected persons) under the State's law of private nuisance, or by the State under its complementary power to abate nuisances that affect the public generally, or otherwise.[16]

On this analysis, the owner of a lake bed, for example, would not be entitled to compensation when he is denied the requisite permit to engage in a landfilling operation that would have the effect of flooding others' land. Nor the corporate owner of a nuclear generating plant, when it is directed to remove all improvements from its land upon discovery that the plant sits astride an earthquake fault. Such regulatory action may well have the effect of eliminating the land's only economically productive use, but it does not proscribe a productive use that was previously permissible under relevant property and nuisance principles. The use of these properties for what are now expressly prohibited purposes was *always* unlawful, and (subject to other constitutional limitations) it was open to the State at any point to make the implication of those background principles of nuisance and property law explicit. See Michelman, Property, Utility, and Fairness, Comments on the Ethical Foundations of "Just Compensation" Law, 80 Harv. L. Rev. 1165, 1239–1241 (1967). In light of our traditional resort to "existing rules or understandings that stem from an independent source such as state law" to define the range of interests that qualify for protection as "property" under the Fifth (and Fourteenth) amendments, *Board of Regents of State Colleges* v. *Roth*, 408 U. S. 564, 577 (1972); see, *e.g.*, *Ruckelshaus* v. *Monsanto Co.*, 467 U. S. 986, 1011–1012 (1984); *Hughes* v. *Washington*, 389 U. S. 290, 295 (1967) (Stewart, J., concurring), this recognition that the Takings Clause does not require compensation when an owner is barred from putting land to a use that is proscribed by those "existing rules or understandings" is surely unexceptional. When, however, a regulation that declares "off-limits" all economically productive or beneficial uses of land goes beyond what the relevant background principles would dictate, compensation must be paid to sustain it.[17]

The "total taking" inquiry we require today will ordinarily entail (as the application of state nuisance law ordinarily entails) analysis of, among other things, the degree of harm to public lands and resources, or adjacent private property, posed by the claimant's proposed activities, see, *e.g.*, Restatement (Second) of Torts §§826, 827, the social value of the claimant's activities and their suitability to the locality in question, see, *e.g.*, *id.*, §§828(a) and (b), 831, and the relative ease with which the alleged harm can be avoided through measures taken by the claimant and the government (or adjacent private landowners) alike, see, *e.g.*, *id.*, §§827(e), 828(c), 830. The fact that a particular use has long been engaged in by similarly situated owners ordinarily imports a lack of any common-law prohibition (though changed circumstances or new knowledge may make what was previously permissible no longer so, see Restatement (Second) of Torts, *supra*, §827, comment *g*. So also does the fact that other landowners, similarly situated, are permitted to continue the use denied to the claimant.

It seems unlikely that common-law principles would have prevented the erection of any habitable or productive improvements on petitioner's land; they rarely support prohibition of the "essential use" of land, *Curtin v. Benson*, 222 U. S. 78, 86 (1911). The question, however, is one of state law to be dealt with on remand. We emphasize that to win its case South Carolina must do more than proffer the legislature's declaration that the uses Lucas desires are inconsistent with the public interest, or the conclusory assertion that they violate a common-law maxim such as *sic utere tuo ut alienum non laedas*. As we have said, a "State, by *ipse dixit*, may not transform private property into public property without compensation . . . ." *Webb's Fabulous Pharmacies, Inc.* v. *Beckwith*, 449 U. S. 155, 164 (1980). Instead, as it would be required to do if it sought to restrain Lucas in a common-law action for public nuisance, South Carolina must identify background principles of nuisance and property law that prohibit the uses he now intends in the circumstances in which the property is presently found. Only on this showing can the State fairly claim that, in proscribing all such beneficial uses, the Beachfront Management Act is taking nothing.[18]

* * *

The judgment is reversed and the cause remanded for proceedings not inconsistent with this opinion.

So ordered.

[1]This specialized historical method of determining the baseline applied because the Beachwood East subdivision is located adjacent to a so-called "inlet erosion zone" (defined in the Act to mean "a segment of shoreline along or adjacent to tidal inlets which is influenced directly by the inlet and its associated shoals," S. C. Code §48–39–270(7) (Supp. 1988)) that is "not stabilized by jetties, terminal groins, or other

structures," §48–39–280(A)(2). For areas other than these unstabilized inlet erosion zones, the statute directs that the baseline be established "along the crest of the primary oceanfront sand dune." §48–39–280(A)(1).

[2]The Act did allow the construction of certain nonhabitable improvements, *e.g.*, "wooden walkways no larger in width than six feet," and "small wooden decks no larger than one hundred forty-four square feet." §§48–39–290(A)(1) and (2) (Supp. 1988).

[3] JUSTICE BLACKMUN insists that this aspect of Lucas's claim is "not justiciable," *post*, at 7, because Lucas never fulfilled his obligation under *Williamson County Regional Planning Comm'n* v. *Hamilton Bank of Johnson City*, 473 U. S. 172 (1985), to "submi[t] a plan for development of [his] property" to the proper state authorities. *Id.*, at 187. See *post*, at 8. But such a submission would have been pointless, as the Council stipulated below that no building permit would have been issued under the 1988 Act, application or no application. Record 14 (stipulations). Nor does the peculiar posture of this case mean that we are without Article III jurisdiction, as JUSTICE BLACKMUN apparently believes, see *post*, at 7, and n. 5. Given the South Carolina Supreme Court's dismissive foreclosure of further pleading and adjudication with respect to the pre-1990 component of Lucas's taking claim, it is appropriate for us to address that component as if the case were here on the pleadings alone. Lucas properly alleged injury-in-fact in his complaint, see App. to Pet. for Cert. 154 (complaint); *id.*, at 156 (asking "damages for the temporary taking of his property" from the date of the 1988 Act's passage to "such time as this matter is finally resolved"). No more can reasonably be demanded. Cf. *First English Evangelical Lutheran Church of Glendale* v. *County of Los Angeles*, 482 U. S. 304, 312–313 (1987). JUSTICE BLACKMUN finds it "baffling," *post*, at 8, n. 5, that we grant standing here, whereas "just a few days ago, in *Lujan* v. *Defenders of Wildlife*, 504 U. S. ___ (1992)," we denied standing. He sees in that strong evidence to support his repeated imputations that the Court "presses" to take this case, *post*, at 1, is "eager to decide" it, *post*, at 10, and is unwilling to "be denied," *post*, at 7. He has a point: The decisions are indeed

very close in time, yet one grants standing and the other denies it. The distinction, however, rests in law rather than chronology. *Lujan*, since it involved the establishment of injury-in-fact at the *summary judgment stage*, required specific facts to be adduced by sworn testimony; had the same challenge to a generalized allegation of injury-in-fact been made at the pleading stage, it would have been unsuccessful.

[4] In that case, the Court of Appeals for the Fourth Circuit reached the merits of a takings challenge to the 1988 Beachfront Management Act identical to the one Lucas brings here even though the Act was amended, and the special permit procedure established, while the case was under submission. The court observed:

"The enactment of the 1990 Act during the pendency of this appeal, with its provisions for special permits and other changes that may affect the plaintiffs, does not relieve us of the need to address the plaintiffs' claims under the provisions of the 1988 Act. Even if the amended Act cured all of the plaintiffs' concerns, the amendments would not foreclose the possibility that a taking had occurred during the years when the 1988 Act was in effect." *Esposito* v. *South Carolina Coastal Council*, 939 F. 2d 165, 168 (CA4 1991).

[5] JUSTICE BLACKMUN states that our "intense interest in Lucas' plight . . . would have been more prudently expressed by vacating the judgment below and remanding for further consideration in light of the 1990 amendments" to the Beachfront Management Act. *Post*, at 10, n. 7. That is a strange suggestion, given that the South Carolina Supreme Court rendered its categorical disposition in this case *after* the Act had been amended, and *after* it had been invited to consider the effect of those amendments on Lucas's case. We have no reason to believe that the justices of the South Carolina Supreme Court are any more desirous of using a narrower ground now than they were then; and neither "prudence" nor any other principle of judicial restraint requires that we remand to find out whether they have changed their mind.

[6] We will not attempt to respond to all of JUSTICE BLACKMUN's mistaken citation of case precedent. Characteristic of its nature

is his assertion that the cases we discuss here stand merely for the proposition "that proof that a regulation does *not* deny an owner economic use of his property is sufficient to defeat a facial taking challenge" and not for the point that "*denial* of such use is sufficient to establish a taking claim regardless of any other consideration." *Post*, at 15, n. 11. The cases say, repeatedly and unmistakably, that "'[t]he test to be applied in considering [a] facial [takings] challenge is fairly straightforward. A statute regulating the uses that can be made of property *effects a taking if it "denies an owner economically viable use of his land."'" Keystone*, 480 U. S., at 495 (quoting *Hodel*, 452 U. S., at 295–296 (quoting *Agins*, 447 U. S., at 260)) (emphasis added).

JUSTICE BLACKMUN describes that rule (which we do not invent but merely apply today) as "alter[ing] the long-settled rules of review" by foisting on the State "the burden of showing [its] regulation is not a taking." *Post*, at 11, 12. This is of course wrong. Lucas had to do more than simply file a lawsuit to establish his constitutional entitlement; he had to show that the Beachfront Management Act denied him economically beneficial use of his land. Our analysis presumes the unconstitutionality of state land-use regulation only in the sense that *any* rule-with-exceptions presumes the invalidity of a law that violates it—for example, the rule generally prohibiting content-based restrictions on speech. See, *e.g.*, *Simon & Schuster, Inc.* v. *New York Crime Victims Board*, 502 U. S. ___, ___ (slip op., at 8) (1991) ("A statute is presumptively inconsistent with the First Amendment if it imposes a financial burden on speakers because of the content of their speech"). JUSTICE BLACKMUN's real quarrel is with the substantive standard of liability we apply in this case, a long-established standard we see no need to repudiate.

⁷ Regrettably, the rhetorical force of our "deprivation of all economi- cally feasible use" rule is greater than its precision, since the rule does not make clear the "property interest" against which the loss of value is to be measured. When, for example, a regulation requires a developer to leave 90% of a rural tract in its natural state, it is unclear whether we would

analyze the situation as one in which the owner has been deprived of all economically beneficial use of the burdened portion of the tract, or as one in which the owner has suffered a mere diminution in value of the tract as a whole. (For an extreme—and, we think, unsupportable—view of the relevant calculus, see *Penn Central Transportation Co.* v. *New York City*, 42 N. Y. 2d 324, 333–334, 366 N. E. 2d 1271, 1276–1277 (1977), aff'd, 438 U. S. 104 (1978), where the state court examined the diminution in a particular parcel's value produced by a municipal ordinance in light of total value of the taking claimant's other holdings in the vicinity.) Unsurprisingly, this uncertainty regarding the composition of the denominator in our "deprivation" fraction has produced inconsistent pronouncements by the Court. Compare *Pennsylvania Coal Co.* v. *Mahon*, 260 U. S. 393, 414 (1922) (law restricting subsurface extraction of coal held to effect a taking), with *Keystone Bituminous Coal Assn.* v. *DeBenedictis*, 480 U. S. 470, 497–502 (1987) (nearly identical law held not to effect a taking); see also *id.*, at 515–520 (REHNQUIST, C.J., dissenting); Rose, *Mahon* Reconstructed: Why the Takings Issue is Still a Muddle, 57 S. Cal. L. Rev. 561, 566–569 (1984). The answer to this difficult question may lie in how the owner's reasonable expectations have been shaped by the State's law of prop- erty— *i. e.*, whether and to what degree the State's law has accorded legal recognition and protection to the particular interest in land with respect to which the takings claimant alleges a diminution in (or elimination of) value. In any event, we avoid this difficulty in the present case, since the "interest in land" that Lucas has pleaded (a fee simple interest) is an estate with a rich tradition of protection at common law, and since the South Carolina Court of Common Pleas found that the Beachfront Management Act left each of Lucas's beachfront lots without economic value.

[8]JUSTICE STEVENS criticizes the "deprivation of all economically beneficial use" rule as "wholly arbitrary", in that "[the] landowner whose property is diminished in value 95% recovers nothing," while the landowner who suffers a complete elimination of value "recovers the land's full value." *Post*, at 4.

This analysis errs in its assumption that the landowner whose deprivation is one step short of complete is not entitled to compensation. Such an owner might not be able to claim the benefit of our categorical formulation, but, as we have acknowledged time and again, "[t]he economic impact of the regulation on the claimant and ... the extent to which the regulation has interfered with distinct investment-backed expectations" are keenly relevant to takings analysis generally. *Penn Central Transportation Co.* v. *New York City*, 438 U. S. 104, 124 (1978). It is true that in at least *some* cases the landowner with 95% loss will get nothing, while the landowner with total loss will recover in full. But that occasional result is no more strange than the gross disparity between the landowner whose premises are taken for a highway (who recovers in full) and the landowner whose property is reduced to 5% of its former value by the highway (who recovers nothing). Takings law is full of these "all-or-nothing" situations.

JUSTICE STEVENS similarly misinterprets our focus on "developmental" uses of property (the uses proscribed by the Beachfront Management Act) as betraying an "assumption that the only uses of property cognizable under the Constitution are *developmental* uses." *Post*, at 5, n. 3. We make no such assumption. Though our prior takings cases evince an abiding concern for the productive use of, and economic investment in, land, there are plainly a number of noneconomic interests in land whose impairment will invite exceedingly close scrutiny under the Takings Clause. See, *e.g.*, *Loretto* v. *Teleprompter Manhattan CATV Corp.*, 458 U. S. 419, 436 (1982) (interest in excluding strangers from one's land).

[9]This finding was the premise of the Petition for Certiorari, and since it was not challenged in the Brief in Opposition we decline to entertain the argument in respondent's brief on the merits, see Brief for Respondent 45–50, that the finding was erroneous. Instead, we decide the question presented under the same factual assumptions as did the Supreme Court of South Carolina. See *Oklahoma City* v. *Tuttle*, 471 U. S. 808, 816 (1985).

[10] The legislature's express findings include the following:

"The General Assembly finds that:

"(1) The beach/dune system along the coast of South Carolina is extremely important to the people of this State and serves the following functions:

"(a) protects life and property by serving as a storm barrier which dissipates wave energy and contributes to shoreline stability in an economical and effective manner;

"(b) provides the basis for a tourism industry that generates approximately two-thirds of South Carolina's annual tourism industry revenue which constitutes a significant portion of the state's economy. The tourists who come to the South Carolina coast to enjoy the ocean and dry sand beach contribute significantly to state and local tax revenues;

"(c) provides habitat for numerous species of plants and animals, several of which are threatened or endangered. Waters adjacent to the beach/dune system also provide habitat for many other marine species;

"(d) provides a natural health environment for the citizens of South Carolina to spend leisure time which serves their physical and mental well-being.

"(2) Beach/dune system vegetation is unique and extremely important to the vitality and preservation of the system.

"(3) Many miles of South Carolina's beaches have been identified as critically eroding.

"(4) . . . [D]evelopment unwisely has been sited too close to the [beach/dune] system. This type of development has jeopardized the stability of the beach/dune system, accelerated erosion, and endangered adjacent property. It is in both the public and private interests to protect the system from this unwise development.

"(5) The use of armoring in the form of hard erosion control devices such as seawalls, bulkheads, and rip-rap to protect erosion-threatened structures adjacent to the beach has not proven effective. These armoring devices have given a false sense of security to beachfront property owners. In reality, these hard structures, in many instances, have increased the vulnerability of beachfront property to damage from wind and waves while contributing to the deterioration and loss of the dry sand beach which is so important to the tourism industry.

"(6) Erosion is a natural process which becomes a significant problem for man only when structures are erected in close proximity to the beach/dune system. It is in both the public and private interests to afford the beach/dune system space to accrete and erode in its natural cycle. This space can be provided only by discouraging new construction in close proximity to the beach/dune system and encouraging those who have erected structures too close to the system to retreat from it.

"(8) It is in the state's best interest to protect and to promote increased public access to South Carolina's beaches for out-of-state tourists and South Carolina residents alike." S. C. Code §48–39–250 (Supp. 1991).

[11]In the present case, in fact, some of the "[South Carolina] legislature's 'findings'" to which the South Carolina Supreme Court purported to defer in characterizing the purpose of the Act as "harm-preventing," 304 S. C. 376, 385, 404 S. E. 2d 895, 900 (1991), seem to us phrased in "benefit-conferring" language instead. For example, they describe the importance of a construction ban in enhancing
"South Carolina's annual tourism industry revenue," S. C. Code §48–39– 250(1)(b) (Supp. 1991), in "provid[ing] habitat for numerous species of plants and animals, several of which are threatened or endangered," §48–39–250(1)(c), and in "provid[ing] a natural healthy environment for the citizens of South Carolina to spend leisure time which serves their physical and mental well-being." §48–39–250(1)(d). It would be pointless to make the outcome of this case hang upon this terminology, since the same interests could readily be described in "harm-preventing" fashion.

JUSTICE BLACKMUN, however, apparently insists that we *must* make the outcome hinge (exclusively) upon the South Carolina Legislature's other, "harm-preventing" characterizations, focusing on the declaration that "prohibitions on building in front of the setback line are necessary to protect people and property from storms, high tides, and beach erosion." *Post*, at 6.

He says "[n]othing in the record undermines [this]

assessment," *ibid.*, apparently seeing no significance in the fact that the statute permits owners of *existing* structures to remain (and even to rebuild if their structures are not "destroyed beyond repair," S. C. Code Ann. §48–39–290(B)), and in the fact that the 1990 amendment authorizes the Council to issue permits for new construction in violation of the uniform prohibition, see S. C. Code §48–39–290(D)(1) (Supp. 1991).

[12] In JUSTICE BLACKMUN's view, even with respect to regulations that deprive an owner of all developmental or economically beneficial land uses, the test for required compensation is whether the legislature has recited a harm-preventing justification for its action. See *post*, at 5, 13–17. Since such a justification can be formulated in practically every case, this amounts to a test of whether the legislature has a stupid staff. We think the Takings Clause requires courts to do more than insist upon artful harm-preventing characterizations.

[13] *E.g.*, *Mugler* v. *Kansas*, 123 U. S. 623 (1887) (prohibition upon use of a building as a brewery; other uses permitted); *Plymouth Coal Co.* v. *Pennsylvania*, 232 U. S. 531 (1914) (requirement that "pillar" of coal be left in ground to safeguard mine workers; mineral rights could otherwise be exploited); *Reinman* v. *Little Rock*, 237 U. S. 171 (1915) (declaration that livery stable constituted a public nuisance; other uses of the property permitted); *Hadacheck* v. *Sebastian*, 239 U. S. 394 (1915) (prohibition of brick manufacturing in residential area; other uses permitted); *Goldblatt* v. *Hempstead*, 369 U. S. 590 (1962) (prohibition on excavation; other uses permitted).

[14] Drawing on our First Amendment jurisprudence, see, *e.g.*, *Employment Division, Department of Human Resources of Oregon* v. *Smith*, 494 U. S. 872, 878–879 (1990), JUSTICE STEVENS would "loo[k] to the *generality* of a regulation of property" to determine whether compensation is owing. *Post*, at 12. The Beachfront Management Act is general, in his view, because it "regulates the use of the coastline of the entire state." *Post*, at 14. There may be some validity to the principle JUSTICE STEVENS proposes, but it does not properly apply to the present case. The equivalent of a law of general application that inhibits the practice of religion without being aimed at religion, see *Oregon*

v. *Smith*, *supra*, is a law that destroys the value of land without being aimed at land. Perhaps such a law—the generally applicable criminal prohibition on the manufacturing of alcoholic beverages challenged in *Mugler* comes to mind—cannot constitute a compensable taking. See 123 U. S., at 655–656. But a regulation *specifically directed to land use* no more acquires immunity by plundering landowners generally than does a law specifically directed at religious practice acquire immunity by prohibiting all religions. JUSTICE STEVENS' approach renders the Takings Clause little more than a particularized restatement of the Equal Protection Clause.

[15] After accusing us of "launch[ing] a missile to kill a mouse," *post*, at 1, JUSTICE BLACKMUN expends a good deal of throw-weight of his own upon a noncombatant, arguing that our description of the "understanding" of land ownership that informs the Takings Clause is not supported by early American experience. That is largely true, but entirely irrelevant. The practices of the States *prior* to incorporation of the Takings and Just Compensation Clauses, see *Chicago, B. & Q. R. Co.* v. *Chicago*, 166 U. S. 226 (1897)—which, as JUSTICE BLACKMUN acknowledges, occasionally included *outright physical appropriation* of land without compensation, see *post*, at 22—were out of accord with *any* plausible interpretation of those provisions. JUSTICE BLACKMUN is correct that early constitutional theorists did not believe the Takings Clause embraced regulations of property at all, see *post*, at 23, and n. 23, but even he does not suggest (explicitly, at least) that we renounce the Court's contrary conclusion in *Mahon*. Since the text of the Clause can be read to encompass regulatory as well as physical deprivations (in contrast to the text originally proposed by Madison, see Speech Proposing Bill of Rights (June 8, 1789), in 12 J. Madison, The Papers of James Madison 201 (C. Hobson, R. Rutland, W. Rachal, & J. Sisson ed. 1979) ("No person shall be . . . obliged to relinquish his property, where it may be necessary for public use, without a just compensation"), we decline to do so as well.

[16]The principal "otherwise" that we have in mind is litigation absolving the State (or private parties) of liability for the

destruction of "real and personal property, in cases of actual necessity, to prevent the spreading of a fire" or to forestall other grave threats to the lives and property of others. *Bowditch* v. *Boston*, 101 U. S. 16, 18–19 (1880); see *United States* v. *Pacific Railroad*, 120 U. S. 227, 238–239 (1887).

[17] Of course, the State may elect to rescind its regulation and thereby avoid having to pay compensation for a permanent deprivation. See *First English Evangelical Lutheran Church*, 482 U. S., at 321. But "where the [regulation has] already worked a taking of all use of property, no subsequent action by the government can relieve it of the duty to provide compensation for the period during which the taking was effective." *Ibid.*

[18] JUSTICE BLACKMUN decries our reliance on background nuisance principles at least in part because he believes those principles to be as manipulable as we find the "harm prevention"/"benefit conferral" dichotomy, see *post*, at 20–21. There is no doubt some leeway in a court's interpretation of what existing state law permits—but not remotely as much, we think, as in a legislative crafting of the reasons for its confiscatory regulation. We stress that an affirmative decree eliminating all economically beneficial uses may be defended only if an *objectively reasonable application* of relevant precedents would exclude those beneficial uses in the circumstances in which the land is presently found.

APPENDIX 2

SYLLABUS

NOTE: Where it is feasible, a syllabus (headnote) will be released, as is being done in connection with this case, at the time the opinion is issued. The syllabus constitutes no part of the opinion of the Court but has been prepared by the Reporter of Decisions for the convenience of the reader. See *United States* v. *Detroit Lumber Co.,* 200 U. S. 321, 337.

SUPREME COURT OF THE UNITED STATES

Syllabus

LUCAS *v.* SOUTH CAROLINA COASTAL COUNCIL

CERTIORARI TO THE SUPREME COURT OF SOUTH CAROLINA

No. 91–453. Argued March 2, 1992—Decided June 29, 1992

In 1986, petitioner Lucas bought two residential lots on a South Carolina barrier island, intending to build single-family homes such as those on the immediately adjacent parcels. At that time, Lucas's lots were not subject to the State's coastal zone building permit requirements. In 1988, however, the state legislature enacted the Beachfront Management Act, which barred Lucas from erecting any permanent habitable structures on his parcels. He filed suit against respondent state agency, contending that, even though the Act may have been a lawful exercise of the State's police power, the ban on construction deprived him of all "economically viable use" of his property and therefore effected a "taking" under the Fifth and Fourteenth Amendments that required the payment of just compensation. See, *e. g., Agins* v. *Tiburon,* 447 U.S. 255, 261. The state trial court agreed, finding that the ban rendered Lucas's parcels "valueless," and entered an award exceeding $1.2 million. In reversing, the State Supreme Court held itself bound, in light of Lucas's failure to attack the Act's validity, to accept the legislature's "uncontested . . . findings" that new construction in the coastal zone threatened a valuable public resource. The court ruled that, under the *Mugler* v. *Kansas,* 123 U.S. 623, line of cases, when a regulation is designed to prevent "harmful or noxious uses" of property akin to public nuisances, no compensation is owing under the Takings Clause regardless of the regulation's effect on the property's value.

LUCAS VS. THE GREEN MACHINE

Held:

1.Lucas's takings claim is not rendered unripe by the fact that he may yet be able to secure a special permit to build on his property under an amendment to the Act passed after briefing and argument before the State Supreme Court, but prior to issuance of that court's opinion. Because it declined to rest its judgment on ripeness grounds, preferring to dispose of the case on the merits, the latter court's decision precludes, both practically and legally, any takings claim with respect to Lucas's preamendment deprivation. Lucas has properly alleged injury-in-fact with respect to this preamendment deprivation, and it would not accord with sound process in these circumstances to insist that he pursue the late-created procedure before that component of his takings claim can be considered ripe. Pp.5–8.

2.The State Supreme Court erred in applying the "harmful or noxious uses" principle to decide this case. Pp.8–26.

(a)Regulations that deny the property owner all "economically viable use of his land" constitute one of the discrete categories of regulatory deprivations that require compensation without the usual case-specific inquiry into the public interest advanced in support of the restraint. Although the Court has never set forth the justification for this categorical rule, the practical—and economic—equivalence of physically appropriating and eliminating all beneficial use of land counsels its preservation. Pp.8–13.

(b)A review of the relevant decisions demonstrates that the "harmful or noxious use" principle was merely this Court's early formulation of the police power justification necessary to sustain (without compensation) *any* regulatory diminution in value; that the distinction between regulation that "prevents harmful use" and that which "confers benefits" is difficult, if not impossible, to discern on an objective, value-free basis; and that, therefore, noxious-use logic cannot be the basis for departing from this Court's categorical rule that total regulatory takings must be compensated. Pp.14–21.

(c)Rather, the question must turn, in accord with this Court's "takings" jurisprudence, on citizens' historic understandings regarding the content of, and the State's power over, the "bundle of rights" that they acquire when they take title to property. Because it is not consistent with the historical compact embodied in the Takings Clause that title to real estate is held subject to the State's subsequent decision to eliminate all economically beneficial use, a regulation having that effect cannot be newly decreed, and sustained, without compensation's being paid the owner. However, no compensation is owed—in this setting as with all takings claims—if the State's affirmative decree simply makes explicit what already inheres in the title itself, in the restrictions that background principles of the State's law of property and nuisance already place upon land ownership. Cf. *Scranton* v. *Wheeler,* 179 U.S. 141, 163. Pp.21–25.

(d)Although it seems unlikely that common-law principles would have prevented the erection of any habitable or productive improvements on Lucas's land, this state-law question must be dealt with on remand. To win its case, respondent cannot simply proffer the legislature's declaration that the uses Lucas desires are inconsistent with the public interest, or the conclusory assertion that they violate a common-law maxim such as *sic utere tuo ut alienum non laedas,* but must identify background principles of nuisance and property law that prohibit the uses Lucas now intends in the property's present circumstances. P.26.

304 S.C. 376, 404 S.E.2d 895, reversed and remanded.

SCALIA, J., delivered the opinion of the Court, in which REHNQUIST, C. J., and WHITE, O'CONNOR, and THOMAS, JJ., joined. KENNEDY, J., filed an opinion concurring in the judgment. BLACKMUN, J., and STEVENS, J., filed dissenting opinions. SOUTER, J., filed a separate statement.

Index

Symbols

LUCAS VS. THE GREEN MACHINE

Liberty 8
Liberty, and the individual 7
Limited government. *See Private property*
Locklair, Jerry 83
Louisville Slugger *17*
Lucas and Gov. Edwards 24
Lucas, and Howe 104
Lucas, April 84, 165, 186
Lucas case 130, 154, 195.
    See also Beachfront Management Act
Lucas, David 104, 110, 115, 116, 124, 153, 155, 159, 181, 246, 247, 252, 256.
    See also American protest; Beachfront Management Act; "Mugler" Rule
"Lucas Environmental Park" 252
Lucas, Martha 20
Lucas property and accretion 116
Lucas v. South Carolina Coastal Council 98, 176, 191, 195, 196, 223
Lucas, W.D. 34
Lucrative litigation *244*

M

Mafia-like tactics 261
Martin d-28 guitar *18*
Martin Magic *19*
Marx, Karl 259
Master of Bovine Scatology *236*
McNair Firm 165
Misguided bureaucrats 8
Money making scheme *244*
Mugler v. Kansas 199
Murrel's Inlet *15, 16, 18*

N

Nashville *15*
New environmental industry 262
Newsmedia 93, 176, 178, 183, 220, 262, 271
"Nimbys" 258
"Nolan Case" 169

P

Pacific Legal Defense Fund *165*, 168
Paine, Thomas 41
Paterson, Larry R. 151
Patterson, Judge 97, 141, 142.
    See also Environmentalists: Media
Pelon, Roger 220. *See also* Cato Institute
Pennsylvania Coal Co v. Mahon 200, 205
People and power 9
Philadelphia *21*
Poland *238*
Police 158

Police state 152, 158, 174
Power
83, 92, 149, 153, 157, 174, 182, 203, 212, 221, 224, 252, 260, 261, 262, 270.
    See also Abuse of power; American protest; Environmentalists; Environmentalists: Media; Freedom; Government intervention; Government regulation; Landowners; Police
Power, and government 213
Power, and prejudice 157
Power, and progress 267
Private property 8, 259, 272.
    See also communism; *governmental powers, resistance to*; Individual freedom; *Individual liberty*
Privilege 7
Property rights *79, 168, 178, 185*, 190, 191, 194, 210, 214, 224, 237, 266.
    See also American Dream; Analysis/law; Communism; *Fifth Amendment*; governmental powers, resistance to; *Individual freedom*; Kennedy's philosophy; Scalia's philosophy; Small business; Zoning
Property rights, and Bush Administration *184*
Property rights, and Fifth Amendment *88*
Property rights, and freedom *160*
Property rights, and Pacific Legal Defense Fund *165*
Property rights, basic *79*
Property rights movement 259.
    See also American Dream
Property rights opponents 232
Property rights protection 270
Property rights rulings *168*
Property rights, see Epstein 185
Public danger 201
Public response 164, 180, 223, 224, 229, 257
Publicity 59, 222, 227
Publicity battle 92
Publicity war 150
Pursuit of happiness *9*

R

Reagan, Ronald 67
Rebel Yell *16*
Reconstruction *15, 20*
"Regulatory taking" 153
Right to own 8
Right to private property 7
Right to use 8
Rights, violation of 8
Ripeness issue 209
"Rocky Top" *12*

The Council
on Property Rights

Property Rights
Foundation of
American Freedom

Our American democracy is <u>built</u> on respect for property rights.

The Founding Fathers believed that property rights served as a <u>bulwark against government</u>. They wrote the "Takings Clause" of the Fifth Amendment of the U.S. Constitution:

> *"... nor shall private property be taken for*
> *public use, without just compensation."*

David Lucas, a homebuilder, was told he could not build houses on his land, yet he was denied compensation. Lucas sued. The United States Supreme Court agreed with Lucas: he deserved compensation.

The Lucas case has ignited a firestorm across the nation. Now property owners are teaming up to fight <u>governmental encroachments on private property rights</u> in the courts, Congress, and statehouses.

Become a member of the Council on Property Rights. Your generous contributions to the Council will be used to influence legislation and <u>are not</u> tax-deductible. To obtain membership (or to request additional information), please send $25 or more to:

The Council on Property Rights
7 Fairway Oaks Lane
Isle of Palms SC 29451
(803) 886-4654 & voice and fax